ANSWER ME THIS!

Helen Zaltzman &
Olly Mann

ANSWER ME
THIS!

ff

First published in 2010
by Faber and Faber Limited
Bloomsbury House,
74–77 Great Russell Street,
London WC1B 3DA

Typeset by Faber and Faber Limited
Printed in the UK by CPI Mackays, Chatham

A CIP record for this book
is available from the British Library

ISBN 978-0-571-26056-0

10 9 8 7 6 5 4 3 2 1

This book is dedicated to all our questioneers, without whom there would be no *Answer Me This!* at all.

Contents

?

Look at that. Isn't it beautiful? The most majestic of all punctuation marks. Add it to the end of a sentence, a slogan or even just a word, and lo, you've just become an *Answer Me This!* Questioneer™.

You're in good company: Questioneers have existed since two minutes after the very dawn of time, when Adam piped up to God, 'Would you mind getting these dinosaurs out of my garden?' Question-answerers have been around for almost as long. In Ancient Greece, the Delphic Oracle sat outside a temple stoned off her tits, doling out gnomic advice that got the likes of Oedipus into no end of trouble.

In 2007, we waded in on this noble tradition of problem-solving by starting our weekly question-answering podcast *Answer Me This!*. As cyberspace's premium question-answerers, our inbox is glutted with thousands of how-tos, what-should-I-dos and would-you-rathers. From these enquiries emerges a picture of the world; and, much like a toddler, the world turns out to be befuddled, inquisitive, and disproportionately obsessed with poo.

Over the years we have answered a dazzling myriad of questions, from 'Who do you think created God?' to 'Can you knob somebody in space?' To us, a question without an answer is like half a snake, or a Happy Meal without heartburn: lacking its natural conclusion. But although we've tackled many great mysteries

? in our podcast, still a great many depths remain unplumbed and facts unturned; and the words 'spin-off' and 'toilet book' began whirling around our brains like wasps at a picnic. Hence you hold in your hands the first ever *Answer Me This!* question compendium. We hope you find it fun, educational and absorbing. Or at least absorbent.

Keep on asking!
Helen and Olly

Had we – and podcasting – been around a bit earlier, the most famous unanswered questions in history would by now be safely tucked up in bed:

'To be or not to be?' – Hamlet, 30, Elsinore

We've always erred on the side of 'to be'. Don't make any hasty decisions, Hamlet: your troubles will seem more bearable after a hot bath, and we're sure your mum is on hand to give you a reassuring cuddle.

If 'not to be' continues to look dangerously tempting, your GP can suggest a course of anti-depressants and refer you to a counsellor. But remember that doctors don't have much time to make their diagnoses these days, Hamlet – so cut the poetry and get to the point.

'Is this the real life? Is this just fantasy?' – Freddie, Brian, Roger and John, 24–29, London

Yes. No. Or vice versa, if you're playing *World of Warcraft*.

'Guitar-shaped swimming pool; gold disc in the toilet . . . Who lives in a house like this?' – Loyd, 50-something, standing in the herbaceous borders

Could it be a venerable politician? An Olympic athlete? One of Britain's favourite retired comedians or actors? No, thicko. It's obviously some shitting soap-star. [Audience applauds.]

21st-Century Blues

Modern life is rubbish, eh, readers? Well, maybe if you were in Blur, or work in a recycling plant. Otherwise it can be quite nice. However, it does come with a flummoxing range of decisions and conundrums that our forebears never had to deal with because they were too busy dodging zeppelins and spinning yarn.

Karina from New Zealand: I've been invited to a 'P'-themed party. What should I go as?

As Prince Harry would tell you – if only you were posh or pretty enough to speak to him – comedy fancy dress can lead to all sorts of problems. It's one thing to squeeze yourself into a corset for a glamorous masked ball; quite another to endure, as Olly once did, five agonising hours with some stripped-off tree bark stapled to your leg in an attempt to approximate Long John Silver.

For ease of mobility, we'd also warn against attending this shindig as a Postbox, the Houses of Parliament, or the Parthenon. Bearing in mind the eggy smell, you should also avoid going as a Passover platter. One should consider the feelings of others, too: if the party's in an army barracks, don't go as a Pacifist. If the birthday girl is allergic, don't dress as a Peanut. If it's a children's party, don't be a Paedophile. Actually, that's good advice generally.

Inevitably several lackwits will take the invitation literally and turn up as the letter P, a Pea, or, in the worst-case scenario, a Puddle of Pee. Think laterally, and try to go as something droll which will simultaneously allow you to look your best. Nobody wants to play tonsil-tennis with someone dressed as a Perineum. A Parentheses costume, however, would require just a pair of cut-out brackets on a headband hanging each side of one's face. A natty little pastry hat would elegantly suggest a Pie. Or, if you have a nice bottom, wear something eyecatching on it to suggest a Peacock.

Whatever she chooses, we'd advise Karina not to get too clever-clever. She shouldn't undermine the party fun by dressing as Psoriasis, or acting Pedantically. And if she writes 'Freedom Is Slavery' in biro on her face, claiming to be a Paradox, her fellow guests are obliged to punch her repeatedly in the face.

Maurice from Milton Keynes: When I was young, I thought Billy Bragg and Melvyn Bragg were the same person. After hearing 'Sexuality' on the radio, and then catching a South Bank Show *on the telly, I got VERY confused. I'm older and wiser now . . . So, answer me this, what two people have YOU thought were the same person?*

Olly, a fragile child, still recalls with horror the afternoons he'd gleefully leap onto the sofa to enjoy unthreatening cartoon series *Mister Benn*, only to be greeted by an episode of the comparatively terrifying *Gentle Ben*, a show about a BIG SCARY BEAR who lived with humans, despite his capacity to murder them in their sleep. Helen was, shamefully, much older when she sat through two hours of *LA Confidential* before realising that Russell Crowe and Kevin Spacey were in fact playing two different characters.

We're never entirely sure which Baldwin brother we're watching at any given time, or who is who in *Hollyoaks*: they all look like slaggy blonde girls, even the boys. However, the most vexing celebrity mix-up we – and, it seems, almost everyone else in Christendom – suffer from is our tendency to confuse ubiquitous middle-aged supporting actor **Bill Pullman** with ubiquitous middle-aged supporting actor **Bill Paxton**. They're both fond of a quiff and playing all-American chaps in extraordinary situations, but we're darned if we can remember which is which, or if either of them is Jeff Daniels.

Can you do any better? Test your skills with our

GUESS THE BILL QUIZ

(answers at the end of the quiz)

1. I am the President in *Independence Day*. To save the world from certain destruction, I've enlisted the elite: an alcoholic, the bloke out of *The Fly*, and the Fresh Prince. I give a rousing speech, declaring to my few remaining fellow Americans that kicking alien ass is comparable to achieving independence from the British in 1776. It's not. **But which Bill am I?**

2. I am Brock Lovett in *Titanic*. I am an intrepid sea-geek in an expensive-looking pod thing. I point at the wreckage of the *Titanic*; I feel sad. Essentially I'm a plot device, allowing the movie to end on a moment of hope and reflection rather than with Jack's frozen corpse sinking to the ocean floor. **But which Bill am I?**

3. I am Bill Harding in *Twister*. I am a TV weatherman in Oklahoma. As if this weren't dull enough, I am married to Helen Hunt. But it's all right – I'm divorcing her for a younger model called Melissa . . . SHIT! Here comes a massive tornado – I'm going to die. Oh, I'm not dead. I am, however, stuck with Helen Hunt. **But which Bill am I?**

4. I am Walter in *Sleepless in Seattle*. It's 1993, therefore Meg Ryan is still hot, and I am engaged to her. I wangled this by giving her a ring from Tiffany's and buying her Dom Perignon in a swanky New York eatery. But because I'm a bit bland, and sneeze a lot, she dumps me for a man she has only ever heard on the radio, blubbing about his dead wife. **But which Bill am I?**

5. I am Fred Haise in *Apollo 13*. I am an astronaut on my way to the moon. Good news: there's zero gravity up here, which is great fun. Bad news: something unexpected happened to my rocket, so unless the RAC come and pick me up from outer space, I'm fucked. **But which Bill am I?**

Could you tell your **Bill** from your **Bill**?

1. Pullman, 2. Paxton, 3. Paxton, 4. Pullman, 5. Paxton

Stuart from East Dulwich: Why on earth is burlesque coming back and what can be done to stop it?

We're as surprised as you, Stuart, that burlesque has managed to carve itself a niche as the stripping it's OK to watch. Without the seedy tang of Lucite platforms, greasy poles and Peter Stringfellow, even women themselves are cheerfully flocking to burlesque clubs: despite all that bra-burning and talk of smiting down any man who dares objectify them, their heads can still be turned by frilly knickers and seamed stockings.

But as feminist pioneers like Emmeline Pankhurst and Ginger Spice would tell you, underneath the ostrich feathers and nipple-tassels, the essentials are the same: punters paying a lady to take her clothes off in provocative fashion, albeit in the style your grandma would have done in her youth. Had she been a stripper, of course.

So why, of all the available sexual stimuli, has burlesque won out? Blame the internet, thanks to which an extensive cache of Californian private parts in brazen postures is available at the click of a mouse. The current generation of schoolkids will never have to resort to raiding recycling bins for porno mags, or poring over the undies section of the Littlewoods catalogue for furtive thrills. But when everything's laid out on a permatanned, silicon-enhanced plate, with all the graphic detail and coquettishness of a gynaecology textbook, a gap in the market appears for suggestiveness, titillation, a bit of sexy mystique. If that can be delivered with a side order of counterculturalism, theatrical props and a load of sequins, so much the better.

Take comfort, Stuart, for like all trends, burlesque is bound to go away sooner or later (although it will probably be succeeded by some other stupid retro revival, like public floggings, polio, or Chartism). Dita von Teese, spearheader of the current Kitsch Stripping movement, is now pushing 40, and being a classy sort of gal, she'll probably want to hang up her waspie before she gets to the point where she needs a special mobility hoist to get out of her trademark martini-glass bubble bath.

Phil: I have recently started downloading classic novels in audiobook format on iTunes. Is it cheating to buy these audiobooks and claim I have read these masterpieces?

It's no more 'cheating', Phil, than reading them in Braille, so long as you are paying attention to every word. But bear in mind that when Tolstoy was penning *Anna Karenina*, he wasn't expecting your iPhone to cut it off at a vital scene so you can receive a lewd text about Miley Cyrus.

Jenny from Coventry: Can you recycle CDs? It feels a bit wrong just to throw them out.

Yes, you can! Your once-cherished copies of *Born To Do It* and *Jive Bunny and the Mastermixers* can be granulated, blended and compounded to create . . . drumroll . . . insulation for electric cables.

It's probably for the best that your CDs are sent off to the industrial mincer: Hoxtonites of the future are hardly going to be yanking at the leash to snap up your second-hand Dido collection. As it happens, we don't think there will ever be a market for vintage CDs – they don't scream 'retro romance' like those old 45s. Recall the potter's wheel scene in *Ghost*, the needle of the jukebox caressing the grooves of the vinyl as the happy couple conjoin to the strains of 'Unchained Melody'. Imagine if Patrick Swayze had de-straddled Demi Moore and crossed the room to press the Play/Pause button on his Aiwa boombox, en route knocking over a vase with his stiffy: all the erotic charge would be lost, they'd have split up soon after, and instead of being shot by a vagrant he'd have gone off to make clay pigeons with another Eighties hottie, such as Kelly LeBrock or Rick Moranis.

Ali in Battersea: Why are estate agents becoming so posh? I live in an area where there are 15 estate agents on one road, and they're all having makeovers. There are lots of revolving displays of posh houses, shiny new signs outside – one of them even has a bar full of drinks, presumably to make you feel more relaxed or something.

Attentive readers will deduce that this question reached our inbox in the early days of *Answer Me This!*, before the global economic recession took hold. However, even now, in this supposed age of austerity, estate agents consider it appropriate to persuade us to buy houses – a transaction of quite some gravity, being the single

If you can't bear to part with your CD collection, reincarnate them in one of the following ways:

- Carry one in your handbag as a handy pocket mirror. Perfect if you have a hole in the middle of your face.
- Thread them together to make some tasteless blinds for your window. Hang with the reflective side facing out to dazzle nosy neighbours.
- Cut off a tiny shard. Next time you go to a gig, pretend you caught the guitarist's plectrum. Then sell it on eBay.
- Fashion your CDs into a mobile to hang over the cot. Perhaps your baby will grow up to be a wedding DJ!
- Emulate Helen's mum and hang them from trees in the garden, to stop birds from flying into the trunks. This is based on the folk wisdom that birds hate digital technology.

most expensive purchase we will make in our lifetimes – in offices that resemble a branch of All Bar One exclusively populated by pinstriped dicks. This has become the template, Ali, due to some highly spurious customer analysis.

The giant plasma screens tuned to Sky News are intended to inspire confidence: here is an organisation with its fingers on the pulse! Whereas any sensible person would consider it distasteful to negotiate contracts worth many thousands of pounds whilst images of disaster-hit shanty towns tower above them. The back-lit fridges full of beer and fizzy water are designed to create the impression that the folks who work here not only know how to bag you a fantastic deal on a three-bedroom semi, but hey, they also appreciate that life isn't all work work work. Yet the one time we absolutely, categorically do not want to be under the influence of alcohol is when signing away our life savings ('Phew, what a night – I just went for a pint after work and woke up with a £600K townhouse!').

Look, estate agents: here's some free advice from the Helen and Olly Branding Consultancy. Most people want to purchase their properties in clean, formal environments staffed by experienced-looking salespeople who are friendly and polite and at least pretend to be honest. That's it. Now take that bottle of Peroni and shove it up your cul-de-sac.

Kimon from East Dulwich: Helen, like you I have an unusual surname. Unlike you, I also have an unusual first name, and often book restaurants under an assumed name to save spelling my name on the phone. Recently, however, I have also started using an assumed name when meeting people I suspect I might not see again. Is this likely to get me into trouble?

Kimon, are you actually the mysterious 'Mr Throbmuscle' Helen met one wild night nine months ago? If so, there's something she needs to tell you . . .

Dan from New Zealand: I've been made redundant. What's the best office equipment to nick before I'm forced out the door?

Start off with spiral-bound notebooks and post-it notes; work up to the photocopier, filing cabinets and door handles.

Will from Islington: Why do Tube carriages have buttons by the side of the doors, as if to make them open, but actually they do nothing?

This feature appears to exist primarily to distinguish which of one's fellow travellers is a tourist. How we seasoned Londoners laugh to ourselves as a country mouse jabs urgently and fruitlessly at the buttons as the train shudders to a halt, unaware the door will open anyway!

Geoff: How come when I googled myself, I found the only other person with the same name photographs naked women for a living and yet I am a Facilities Manager?

It's not like the olden days, Geoff, where all the Coopers were barrel-makers, all the Smiths hammered horseshoes for a living, all the Chandlers made candles and all the Walkers manufactured packets of crisps.* Your name is no longer an accurate indicator of your station in life, which is why Prince is not an actual prince and Sandra Bullock is not an actual bullock.

So why would you assume that you and this other Geoff ought to have a lot in common, when you know full well that you also do not share professions with retired strongman Geoff Capes, Geoff Barrow out of the band Portishead, or tale-telling Geoff Chaucer? Were you in fact on the path to becoming a naked-lady photographer but found the lure of Facilities Management too strong?

You know, if you're really jealous of Other Geoff, it's not too late for a career change; and you could use the name-sharing to your advantage, by co-opting his CV as your own to get a head start in the industry. But beware, when switching jobs from managing facilities to ogling them, your rookie overexcitement

---

* It intrigued us to discover that the surname Kellogg was borne by those who killed hogs for a living – no wonder the family Kellogg later rebelled against their nominal heritage by manufacturing cornflakes for the vegan Seventh Day Adventists.

could give you away, so steady those trembling hands, and be sure to wear some very controlling underpants.

Mark from Liverpool: Why isn't Bonfire Night illegal?

Woah, put down the statute books! What exactly concerns you about this parade of pyromania? That it's inappropriate to have lots of fun commemorating an attempted terrorist atrocity on Parliament by burning an effigy of the alleged culprit? Fair point: Croydon council rejected our application for a Timothy McVeigh summer fayre citing similar concerns.

The pain of events like the Gunpowder Plot inevitably fades as the centuries go by. Those who wish to teach the lessons of the past must find a way to communicate that pain anew, which is why Celine Dion was hired to sing the theme to *Titanic*. It's only because Bonfire Night happens once a year that schoolchildren have ever heard of the Guy Fawkes story. Throughout our cities stand unloved statues and monuments, covered in bird crap and Big Mac wrappers: they're hardly a more effective way of educating people about history.

If your concerns are about public safety – the fact that for four weeks each year any tracksuited twat can stride into Asda and buy a boxful of explosives which they can then fire into people's faces for a laugh – then you have a point. After all, most quaint customs do not require TV safety announcements. Were there a law preventing the widespread sale of fireworks, never again would we have to witness our dads risk life, limb and the herbaceous borders to set off a Roman Candle.

But we see no argument for banning properly organised firework displays. Do you seriously wish to deprive us of our annual opportunity to stand in a wet park, twizzling a sparkler to the sound of local radio presenters reading out the number plates of badly parked cars? Have you no compassion for the hotdog salespeople of North Hertfordshire? Do you really wish to deny Walter Murphy and the Big Apple Band of all those royalty payments? Have a heart, Mark. We Brits are a famously repressed race, and without our annual opportunity to mumble 'Ooh!' and 'Aaah!' at spangles in the sky, we might explode from the pent-up emotion.

Phil from Treorchy: The gym – what's the effing point? I don't mean what's the point in keeping fit, people tell me that's a good idea. But why spend so much money joining the gym?

Phil misunderstands the nature of the transaction that occurs when otherwise sane people set up a direct debit with a supple receptionist in a shell-suit. They are not paying to *use* the gym. They're well aware they could use the stairwell at home for step aerobics, a supermarket trolley instead of a rowing machine, and bags of sugar and flour as dumbbells (then bake a delicious cake afterwards). They are committing their fifty quid a month, even though they can't afford it, because that *in itself* makes them feel better; then, if they ever withdraw their stipend to this temple of pain, they feel an overwhelming sense of having Let Themselves Down. And, as we all know, the only way to put that right is by re-joining the gym.

Once you're a fully paid-up gymnast, there are some lesser-known pleasures to be enjoyed at these iron-pumping torture gardens. The steam room, for instance, allows you to *feel* healthy whilst merely lolling about gossiping and inhaling other people's sweat. Then there's that bank of TVs by the cardio equipment, all tuned to channels you would never normally watch – an efficient way to catch up on all the latest R&B chartbusters. Furthermore, there are unparalleled people-watching opportunities: Olly once witnessed an elderly man fastidiously blow-drying his testicles whilst whistling the theme from *Dynasty*.

Sarah: What do you think of internet relationships?

We think they're good. In fact, taking a cue from many bastions of print media, we're going to transfer all of our relationships to solely online form.

Kirsty: Do the police still use graphology?

If you mean, 'Do the police still employ handwriting experts to analyse documents such as suicide notes, signatures and possible forgeries to determine whether they have been penned by the person to whom they are attributed?', then yes, they do.

Whereas if you mean, 'Do the police use a method of calligraphy-based fortune-telling via which they can ascertain the criminal's character, background and methodology just from the way he or she crosses their Ts?', then no, because graphology has no credible, scientific foundation. Sure, it's amusing to have it done in the crank tent at the local village fete, but you wouldn't expect the coconut shy and 'Guess the weight of the cake' contest to be influential in criminal investigation either.

Anna: having just spent eight hours staring at the backs of heads of 82 English literature students, not even being allowed to read or draw or anything, I now think I may have gone completely mad. I am NEVER EVER agreeing to invigilate exams again. So Helen and Olly, answer me this, and perhaps make me feel better about getting myself into another fine employment-based mess: what's the worst job you have ever had?

You too can be a graphologist! Lesson 1:

Look carefully at the specimen of handwriting below.
What can you conclude from it?

Did you spot the clues?

1 The note is written in blood rather than ink.
2 The letters are jagged and pointy. Like knives!
3 Aside from the 'G', the absence of curved letters
   indicates a sociopathic hatred of women. The writer's
   victims are likely to be female, and treated very
   violently.
4 The words slope down the page to the right, signifying
   that the writer is feeling down.
5 All the double 'L's show the writer is obsessed with the
   Twin Towers.
6 The smiley face over the 'I' in 'AGAIN' shows
   the writer is trying to inject a little humour into
   proceedings.

OLLY: At the tender age of seventeen I was lured by a cavalier temp agency to take a 'secretarial position' (in truth, data entry) in a 'new media company' (newspaper depot) in 'trendy Camden' (industrial estate in King's Cross). The job – Jesus Christ, even describing it makes me depressed – was to input the barcodes of '20p off the *Daily Mail*' vouchers that had been handed in by customers and returned to the depot by newsagents. It was solitary, unsociable work; we weren't allowed to speak to each other, or have the radio on lest we disturb the call centre next door; and the only reason I didn't repeatedly self-harm with the stapler was that I didn't want to ruin my (entirely superfluous) suit and tie.

HELEN: One year after graduating, I lacked any discernible career and, importantly, any income. So I didn't hesitate when a temp agency offered me a seven-week posting with a 'great bunch of people', a phrase which frequently emerges from the mouth of a recruitment agent but, mark me, is never, *ever* true.

The job was in the housing benefit office of a bleak area of East London. My initial duties involved pushing around a little cart full of files, at which I proved so dazzlingly adept that I was soon promoted to determining whether or not the benefit claimants were eligible for free school uniform vouchers. I kept my mind occupied with thoughts of plunging from the fourth-floor windows onto the concrete below; alas, the windows had been glued shut, a visible clue of the council's expectations for employee satisfaction.

The aforementioned great bunch of people turned out to be barely literate, and proud of it: the brightest one was a cocky 15-year-old school-shunner who believed that people breathe through their hearts. The rest had somehow succeeded in making it to middle age, but still managed to send out letters with no verbs in, which must have proved incomprehensible to the non-English-speaking Bangladeshi locals receiving them. I kept quiet that I had a degree. Heck, I kept quiet about the fact I had GCSEs.

Leafing through a case file one day, I discovered the purest exemplar of my colleagues' aversion to thinking. 'Dear Mr Ahmed,' read the photocopied letter at the front of the file. 'I am sorry to inform you that you have been refused housing benefit, on the grounds that you are deceased. Enclosed is a copy of your death certificate.'

Mr Ahmed had not seen fit to reply.

Bas from the Netherlands: I was at the checkout of my local grocery store when a young man with acne came into the store wearing sunglasses. Is it ever OK to wear sunglasses inside?

It's fine, if you are Stevie Wonder. But remember, he enjoys an unusually large quantity of public goodwill.

Mathew: Why do some people, who do not speak Chinese, choose to have Chinese writing on their arms?

Traditionally, calligraphy is a very highly valued art form in Chinese culture, and a prized attribute when making the choice of a suitable husband or wife. That's probably not uppermost in the mind of the tattooee, however, who just believes they will look more worldly and spiritual than if they'd had 'Destiny' inscribed upon their bicep in plain English.

Aside from the obvious drawback of a tatt that is not only a bit pretentious, but rather unoriginal, there's another flaw in this scheme. The likelihood of the clientele having mastered Mandarin is so slim that the tattoo artist, a.k.a. 'skin vandal', can then etch any old Chinese-looking scrawl onto their arms. The customer is none the wiser, until they wear a short-sleeved t-shirt to a dim sum restaurant and the waiters fall about laughing.

We have seen far fewer good tattoos than bad ones. And even the good ones are unlikely to remain good as the inexorable march of time slackens the skin, sprinkles it with freckles and garnishes with sprouting hair. It's really too bad that something about which one should really think long and carefully is something people so often do when they're drunk out of their skulls.

So, before plumping for everlasting decorations, do yourself a lifelong favour and follow our **GOLDEN RULES OF TATTS**:

1 Before you get your tattoo, draw the design upon yourself with a marker pen and walk around with it for at least six months. This technique apes the compulsory preparation for people undergoing gender reassignment surgery, who have to live in their new gender for a period of time before their genitals get permanently remodelled.
2 If opting for a wordy tattoo, check and double-check your spelling. A brief googling of 'tattoo fails' will prove why this is a wise precaution.
3 Don't get a tattoo on any part of your body which would still be showing if you were dressed in a monk's habit.
4 If you can't remember your children's names without them being etched onto your skin, you should be visiting Social Services, not a body artist.

You may think we're being killjoys, but you'll thank us for this advice in a few years' time when you aren't having to have the Playboy bunny logo lasered off your forehead.

Ellie, 13, from Brussels: Why on Earth is the 'R' in Toys'R'Us upside-down?

Actually it's back to front, but we'll take your age and bilingualism into account and forgive you the error. The backwards R in the Toys'Я'Us logo was designed to emulate a child's handwriting: kids often scribble large, topsy-turvy letters, without regard for sense, orientation or calligraphy. The "Я'Us" portion of the name is a punning tribute to the chain's founder, Charles Lazarus. Do you see it? Do you? That's why we're always laughing so hard when we drive through the retail park!

 As a budding shopaholic, I loved nothing more than whiling away a Sunday afternoon in 'Toy Suris' as Mum called it, a reference to the Yiddish for 'hassle'. How happily I skipped across that rainbow threshold in the middle of the joyless industrial estate, eager to splurge my parents' money like a prepubescent desperate housewife. I still recall the full wishlist of toys I was denied – a Space Hopper, the *Neighbours* trivia game, Pop-Up Pirate, an Atari Lynx – but few of the ones I was actually bought. Under Geoffrey the Giraffe's watchful eye, I road-tested everything from a Super NES to Teenage Mutant Hero Turtles rollerskates, and got hooked on the thrill of 'try before you buy'.

One weekend, Dad took me to visit an independent toyshop owned by a mate of his in Watford. Whilst he caught up with his old friend, I was sent to peruse the ▶

shop and choose something I wanted. Unaware that the interactive experience of Toy Suris wasn't *de rigueur* in smaller toyshops, I mounted a battery-powered quadbike, and softly squeezed the accelerator. Seconds later, I was zooming through the shop, out the front door and onto the High Street, slaloming around startled pedestrians at 5mph. I can't remember much of the next fifteen seconds except for my father running behind me shouting something about a brake pedal. I finally crashed into a rubbish bin. Thereafter, I only ever played with toys after we'd got them home. ■

Melvyn in Brighton: do you have any funny/witty suggestions that I could write in birthday cards that are circulated around the office? I get on with everybody, but not great mates. I'm getting fed up writing the same thing, 'Happy Birthday, have a good one' or 'Happy Birthday, have a great day!' etc.

We share your angst, Melvyn; nary a mind in the world doesn't go blank when presented with yet another of those infernal pan-office cards. Our flowchart opposite demonstrates the full gamut of card-quips available.

Phil: When people from the UK go on holiday outside of Western Europe or North America for durations in excess of three weeks, why do they refer to it as 'travelling'? This is particularly prevalent amongst gap-year students. Just because they go to more than one location on their holiday, they're not fucking travelling, they're on holiday! Why do these moronic individuals seem to think they're Indiana Jones!?! Don't they understand that they are on the same

21st-Century Blues

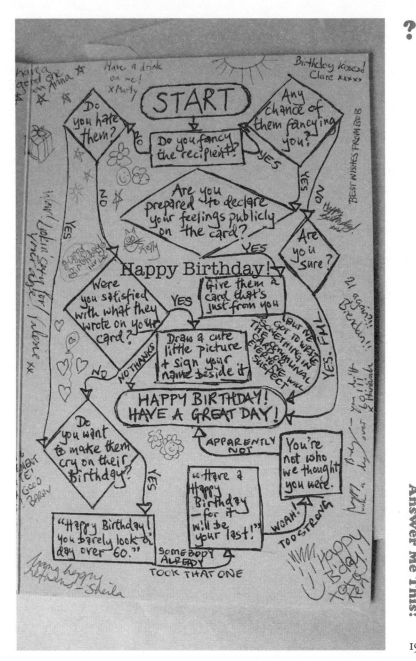

package trip to Africa or Australasia that everyone else their age has been on?

Holidays are for fun. Travelling is not fun, because it usually involves diarrhoea. Travelling is for finding yourself; holidays are for forgetting yourself, because for two weeks a year you want to be that guy who wears loud shirts and only drinks from neon plastic glasses with paper umbrellas and chunks of pineapple sticking out of them.

What's more, going on holiday for six months gives the impression that you are a frivolous person, and gap-year students take themselves far too seriously for that. Travelling, however, is in the venerable tradition of exploration, although Columbus and Magellan never went on a package tour to Goa. The average Don'tcallmetourist wants to give the impression that they're hungry to see as much of the world as possible, each day waking up to a new culture and fresh experience, even though in reality they're waking up in yet another hostel full of noisy Israeli backpackers.

We should try to be kinder to the concept of travelling, for it serves a very noble purpose. It broadens the mind; it bolsters the economy of some of the world's poorer nations; yes yes yes. But most of all, it's a real boon for parents: finally they can get their offspring out of the way, so they can enjoy themselves at last after eighteen years of servitude. Faced with the prospect of a year of their beloved progeny lying all day on the sofa ironically watching *In the Night Garden* whilst guzzling the full fridge inventory, who wouldn't prefer to despatch their children to be pompous in South East Asia?

21st-Century Blues

Helen says:

My youthful rebellion took the form of me shunning the norms for my peer-group, i.e.: I didn't smoke or drink, and I preferred old blues to Britpop. More significantly, I disliked bad lavatories. Hence I decided to spend my gap year not trekking in the Himalayan foothills or teaching English in a remote Ugandan school, but working in an antiquarian bookshop in Tunbridge Wells.

Did I find myself? Mercifully not, but I did find many fantastic books, like *282 Ways of Making a Salad* and *7,000 Words Often Mispronounced*. If I were Dean at the University of Life, these would be set texts.

That's Entertainment!

Here we ponder your pop-culture queries, from the glitz of the silver screen to the clits of online porno. We've got showbiz in our blood, you see. By which we mean we spend a lot of time sitting on our arses watching telly, and Olly looks a bit like Seth Rogen before he got all buff.

Hugo from Stoke Newington: How can I recreate the festival atmosphere in my office, given that I'm not going to any real festivals this year?

Here are our ten top tips to ensure your workplace feels like a fully-fledged festival by summer's end. Make sure you arrive by Thursday night to ensure you get the best desk!

1 Soak your socks in cold water on your way to work.
2 Apply beer as a cologne.
3 Drink chai. Take this moment to remember why you normally drink tea.
4 Drop any food wrappers, tissues and plastic cutlery on the floor and squish them into the carpet with your feet.
5 Reverse the extractor fan in the lavatories so the smell of raw sewage fills the air.
6 Whoop whenever someone mentions the name of the town where your company is based.

7 Allow ninety minutes to walk between the filing cabinet and the photocopier.
8 Play a Coldplay CD loudly in the main office, then put on some Youssou N'Dour, very quietly, in the caretaker's cupboard.
9 Exchange your ergonomic office chair for a log.
10 In staff meetings, make sure all the shortest women in the office stand right behind you, so they can't see anything. Offer to hoist one of them up onto your shoulders, but only if she'll expose her boobs. Then chuck her through the air. If she complains when she hits the floor with a thud, explain that you thought she wanted to go 'meeting surfing'.

Alex and Rosie in Hull: If no one buys a cinema ticket, do they still run the film?

Yes, they do – partly in case the audience arrive late; partly so that the projectionist has something to do and doesn't spend the rest of the day masturbating or stealing the pick 'n' mix.

Lorna: My friend and I have been searching in the park for AGES – why is it that you can't find any decent poets nowadays?

Silly Lorna! Today's poets aren't to be found gaining inspiration from the great outdoors, breeze in their beards and daffodils underfoot – they're all throwing down some rhymes onstage at performance poetry clubs. And the world is no better for it.

Jo in Nairobi: What's the scariest or most disturbing fairy tale?

It's a competitive field, but our money's on 'Hansel and Gretel'. In this litany of social service failures, two innocents are abandoned by their parents, TWICE, left to fend for themselves in a forest, and groomed by a cannibalistic witch. The kids, already in breach of the Countryside Code by littering the woods with bread and pebbles, must then turn to MURDER to escape their candied prison. Although they are spared a jail sentence, following all that trauma they are returned to the very same guardians who so unscrupulously desecrated their childhoods. Surely foster care would have been a better option.

You think such a harrowing story isn't suitable pre-watershed entertainment for our youth? Wrongo! Children are callous, bloodthirsty little fuckers who don't fully understand real pain and misery, or the serious implications of the comic-book violence they so relish. Oh, they might enjoy singing 'Jack and Jill' at mother's knee, but it won't cross their minds that Jack and Jill struggle daily with no running water, that Jack dies of horrific head injuries, and that sexism is so ingrained in their society that no one gives a shit about what happens to Jill.

Children's literature is littered with some of the most distressing and distasteful imagery to be found outside of the Old Testament. The Brothers Grimm's version of 'Cinderella', in which the ugly sisters slice bits off their feet to make the glass slipper fit, is as far removed from the Disney adaptation as *Driller Killer* is from *Heidi*. Meanwhile poor old Rapunzel – named after a type of *lettuce* for God's sake – is locked up when she hits puberty. Adolescence is a chaotic time for any young lady, but doubly troublesome when some meathead clambers up your hair and leaves you pregnant in a one-window bedsit.

Consider the lessons these sadistic stories teach suggestible younglings. If you're a downtrodden girl, your only way out of your rubbish life is to marry some toff you've only met once before and who loves you for your looks alone. If you're a sweet kind mother, you will die very young. If you are a widowed man, you will inevitably marry a gold-digging bitch who overrules you on all matters of childcare. Meanwhile, forget career ambitions: either you're born into wealth, or you win it off a giant.

In summary: *all* fairy tales are disturbing, so if you wish to protect your sprog, you had better make sure they never learn to read.

Vicky from Oxted: I was talking to my friend Harry about Monopoly, and which figurines we favour. He always uses the dog, and I always use the wheelbarrow. Answer me this: which Monopoly figure do you like to use?

Olly is very particular on this point, as he splashed out £40 (£40!) on a Sixtieth Anniversary Limited Edition of Monopoly, which came with little wooden houses instead of plastic ones, its own bespoke range of gold-sprayed playing pieces, and a big red badge saying 'SUCKER!' As you might imagine, Vicky's beloved plastic wheelbarrow is not one of the avatars available in this luxury set; if there were a counter as lowly as a wheelbarrow, it would come in Cath Kidston print, with a little plastic butler to push it for you. Olly's preference is to play as Mr Monopoly himself, Rich Uncle Pennybags; but if *forced* to play your commoners' edition, he would plump for the car, as it provides comfort and convenience, and the congestion charge isn't really an issue when you're snapping up Park Lane properties for £200.

Helen generally dislikes Monopoly for its tendency to bring out the worst in people: one minute you're sitting around having a leisurely Sunday lunch with your family, the next you're ruthlessly shafting each other to bankruptcy. She prefers to play light, simple games like Connect 4, although the gravity which characterises her gameplay would be rather more appropriate for the chess match with Death in *The Seventh Seal* than a glorified version of noughts and crosses.

Monopoly is of course an all-time classic. But it sure needs updating for the twenty-first century (£100 to build a house in Angel Islington? In our dreams!). We suggest:

OLD MONOPOLY

NEW MONOPOLY

'Get out of jail free'

'Get out of going to jail altogether, thanks to prison overcrowding'

The top hat

A Beanie hat

'You have won second prize in a beauty contest! Collect £10'

'You have won second prize in a beauty contest! Collect a voucher for a free boob job, then "accidentally" leak your home-made sex tape on the internet'

The boot

An Ugg boot

'Speeding fine £15'

'Speeding fine £120, or only £60 if you pay within 14 days'

'Advance to Trafalgar Square'

'Advance to Trafalgar Square – oh crap, there's a flashmob! Retreat!'

Build a hotel

Apply to Channel 4 for your hotel-building project to be featured on *Grand Designs*.

'It's your birthday. Receive £10 from each player'

'It's your birthday. Receive 15 greetings on Facebook from people who barely know you, but nothing from your actual friends'

'Go back to Old Kent Road'

'Wait an hour for the night bus outside the big Tesco on Old Kent Road'

Angela in the wilds of Shikoku, Japan: What exactly is a 'bunny boiler'? I've heard it so many times over the years (not aimed at me, of course) that I'm simply too embarrassed to admit that I don't know what it means.

Bless you, Angela. You must have been lost in the wilds of Shikoku since 1987 to have missed the movie *Fatal Attraction*, thanks to which we now have the term 'bunny boiler' to denote a mentally unstable woman into whom you will totally regret sticking your penis.

Back then, Michael Douglas was considered suitable to play sexy characters, because in those days, what women wanted from their celluloid crumpet were bulging eyeballs rather than muscles. Hence in the film, happily-married Michael embarks on a racy affair with Glenn Close, and they have lots of 80s-style sexy sex on the kitchen sink.*

But when Michael attempts to end the affair, the prospect of renouncing his creased and greying genitals drives Glenn Close proper postal, and she embarks on a campaign of revenge which is 100 per cent unlikely to make him want her again. In the film's most memorable scene, Michael's innocent lady wife arrives home one afternoon to find a large saucepan bubbling on the stove. Back in the 1980s, husbands didn't cook, so immediately she knows that someone must have broken into the family homestead – perhaps a proponent of the Slow Food Movement? No! The lid comes off, and bobbing about in the pan's seething depths is . . . her daughter's beloved pet rabbit. Glenn, you see, has boiled the bunny.

With this gesture, we understand how crazy Glenn is striking at the thing Michael values almost as highly as dicking deranged women: his family. Happy families and mental ladies who like

---

* NB: this does not mean *Fatal Attraction* should be classified as a kitchen sink drama. Its similarities to *Look Back in Anger* are negligible.

boffing really don't mix, as Courtney Love has proved time and again. However, we must also consider a more generous interpretation of Glenn's intentions: she might actually be trying to show Michael that she too could be a marvellous little housewife, greeting him after a hard day at the office with a piping-hot supper of rabbit stew. Alas, the stupid wench hasn't even *peeled* the rabbit before putting it into the pot, so the supper is completely inedible. You'll never get a husband like that, Glenn!

Dave from Coventry: *In Formula One, does the 'Formula' part have some scientific meaning?*

No, the 'formula' merely refers to a set of rules to which all participants and cars must comply. For example, no women must be allowed anywhere near the track unless they are TV reporters, and only then if they have the most extraordinary tits known to man. All racing drivers possess a monotone voice, grade-two stubble, and less charisma than their own waxwork. Upon winning the Drivers' Championship, participants must spray a bottle of champagne into their own face in a fit of fizzy self-bukkake, and laugh, laugh, laugh, as if this has never been done before. Crucially, the risk of life-threatening injury – the only reason massive audiences tune in each week – shall never be referenced by any of the competitors, who instead must allude to 'pace', 'momentum', and 'high-performance engineering'.

Alex: *Why are there blank pages at the back of most books? It seems very wasteful and pointless to me.*

Imagine, Alex, a little stack of eight sheets of paper. Go on, it's easy. Then, imagine folding that stack down the middle, so you've got a little booklet. Imagine making a whole lot more of those identical booklets, sewing them together, then slapping an ISBN number on the outside: what would you have? A *book*! Little booklets are what books are made of; and if you don't believe us, you can dissect this one after you've finished reading it.

A booklet made of eight slices of paper equals thirty-two book pages. Count 'em. Therefore, unless an author can eke their text out to an exact multiple of thirty-two pages, inevitably there will be a few spare pages at the end. You can blame maths for that. Bloody maths.

If you find these pages so intolerable, try putting them to good use. Draw a nice picture. Write a pithy review of the just-finished book. Add your own appendices, or a spare index. Scribble secret messages that you don't want the police to find for quite some time. Press some nice wild flowers. Or solve your problems the modern way and buy yourself an e-reader. Sure, they lack many of the useful qualities that old-style books have – books cost far less than several hundred quid, they're perfectly capable of surviving a fall to the pavement or into the bath, they won't conk out in less than a year's time, and they never run out of battery – but you'll not be troubled by these bastard surplus pages any more.

Jamie, in France but not French: Often the last thing you do, sing or write is referred to as your 'swan song'. Why is this so? I have on many occasions tried to tempt a swan into a musical outburst but I have yet to succeed.

It's not you, Jamie; it's the swans. They can't sing a note! The expression is based on a myth, dreamt up by the Swan Exaggeration Board, that there was a legendary strain of swans which remained silent all their lives then, upon their deathnests, emanated a single song of staggering beauty. Yet anyone who has ever been near a lake knows that swans spend their lives emitting

? a cacophony of honking, and their death is your only chance to get a bit of bloody peace and quiet.

Andy from Harold Wood, Essex: Who invented the dance to the Macarena?

The dance to the Macarena was inadvertently invented by Olly whilst he desperately attempted to escape from a party where the song was being played. First he searched for his car keys in the palm of his hands, then in his shirt pocket, then his back pocket, until finally he swivelled round in frustration, realising he had left them in the ignition all along. And lo, as with most things Olly does, the world followed suit.

However, some deniers claim that the dance was created in 1996, three years after Los Del Rio first released the track. When the record label noticed the song's popularity on cruise-ships and in Hell, they duly decided to make a video for it, and commissioned flamenco instructor Mia Frye to construct a straightforward routine which even the drunkest, fattest, most dilapidated of idiots could replicate.

Thanks to Frye's ruthless skills in the field of lowest-common-denominator choreography, the song became the Billboard Chart hit of the summer; her dance became firmly enshrined in the wedding reception repertoire; and more than a decade later, we still instinctively know to get in line and slap our buttocks as soon as we hear those two sun-dried Spaniards serenading slaggy Macarena. Ay-eee!

Sam from New Winton in Scotland: Why do lion tamers use chairs?

Lion tamers need a nice sit-down and a cup of tea as much as the next man! Unless the next man is the ringmaster, who could

That's Entertainment!

usually do with losing a few pounds. Besides, chairs make a surprisingly decent defensive weapon, should the lion decide to go a bit Siegfried and Roy – not as decent as a gun, perhaps, but lions are worth considerably more than tamers, and nobody goes into showbiz for the job security anyway.

The reason they use chairs rather than, say, full body shields, is because big cats are supposedly biologically programmed to hone in on a lone animal and attack it; so if you hold up a chair, they're flummoxed by suddenly having four legs on which to focus. Unable to determine a single target for their bloodlust, they'll back off, confused, and perhaps go and eat a Lion bar instead.

Furthermore, chairs are a normal household object, so the tamers can just bring one in from home rather than having to shell out on something fancy when they've already maxed their credit cards to pay for the bloody lion. Chairs also appear relatively harmless to the viewing public: a normal household object, next to the lion which is very much NOT a normal household object, will barely be noticed at all, much less be identified as an animal-suppressing instrument. Much more palatable than the tinsel-covered crowbars Helen saw thrashing an elephant's leg at a Moscow circus, but, it has to be said, less compellingly kinky.

Andy from Essex: if you could rewrite any book in the whole WORLD, what would it be and what would you change about it?

The Bible. We wouldn't actually change any of the contents; we'd just put a big sticker saying 'DISCLAIMER! Work of fiction' on the cover.

Vicky, aged 15: I just watched the film Lolita *online. Answer me this: WHAT THE FREAKING FUCK? I was in floods of tears at the tragic and powerful ending, when a caption on the screen says they*

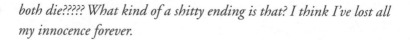

both die?????? What kind of a shitty ending is that? I think I've lost all my innocence forever.

Frankly your innocence was shot to pieces *before* you reached the end of a film about a middle-aged man having sex with his step-daughter.

Acatia: I work in an exotic furniture and candle shop, and every now and then there's a song that comes on which clearly goes 'I want to go to Havana' with a reply from a female voice saying, 'You know you can't go to Havana'. So, please answer me this: why won't she let him go?

Because the conversation is taking place on a picket line protesting the US trade embargo against Cuba.

Charlie from Bristol: Can listening to classical music actually make me cleverer? I am in the middle of my A-levels and am wondering if listening to classical music will make me vastly more intelligent in the next week and a half. Can it?

It's unrealistic to expect anything to make you cleverer in a week and a half – even if you spent the whole time plugged into Wagner's Ring Cycle, glugging back litres of omega 3, and playing speed Sudoku. But don't panic: last-minute cramming has practically nothing to do with intelligence. Firstly, identify which areas of the curriculum completely passed you by, for instance that day you spent gazing down your teacher's cleavage instead of concentrating on *The Crucible*. Then all you need to do is memorise a couple of handy quotations from the relevant edition of *York Notes*; reproduce them under exam conditions; steer the question convincingly towards something you do know about; and hey presto, it's as if you'd been a diligent student all along.

If you want to accompany the process with some Bach piano concertos, we're sure it wouldn't hurt, but for all the difference it'll make, you might as well listen to whatever you like. To ease you through the panic of last-minute revision, we recommend 'Out Of Time' by Blur, 'Under Pressure' by Queen and 'Oh Well, I'll Never Learn' by Morrissey.

Hope from Leicester: When you were younger, did you like the club-bing scene? I just came home early from a night out because I HATE it, but all my uni friends want to do it and I don't know why.

You must be some kind of a Total Square, Hope, not to relish the hours of getting ready to be judged by your peers, the endless lines to get in, the aggressive doormen, the extortionate entry fees, the queue for the bar, the overpriced drinks, the pricks doing coke in the toilets, the vomit on the carpets, the monotonous 'music' at ear-splitting volume, the debased DJs telling you to laaaaaaarge it (whatever that means), the brides-to-be wearing L-plates and wielding cock-shaped whistles as they corner you to lick your face, the noxious BO emanating from the only man dancing anywhere near you, the crying girls blocking every step of every staircase, the shouting into people's ears just to keep up idle conversation, the crippling frustration of missing the last train home by ten minutes because your mate is tonguing someone who's probably still in sixth form, and then, icing on the cake, the night bus crammed with glass-throwing yobs. We're MadFerIt! Wickidwickidwickid! Ayia Napa!

Oh, we fool nobody. As Hope hints in her question, club-bing is mostly a youthful pursuit, and thankfully we are now old enough that we are finally allowed to ignore it. The last time we frequented a nightclub, Tony Blair was still the Prime Minister and Madonna still looked like a human woman. Hang on in there, Hope, and you too will reach the age when one is more regularly invited to nights in with a pizza than nights out spewing up pizza.

Wade from Mansfield: If The Flintstones *is set BC, then why are there Christmas episodes?*

And this bothers you because in all other respects, *The Flintstones* is a bastion of historical accuracy, realistically depicting the peaceful coexistence of fully-evolved humans and Technicolor dinosaurs? Dinosaurs became extinct some 60 million years before the Stone Age, during which the show is set. Fred wears a tie, even though *shirts* haven't even been invented yet, and the only people who wear ties without shirts are Chippendales, who also haven't been invented yet. Fred, Wilma and their daughter Pebbles have all attended the same high school, even though the first co-educational American high school opened in 1833 in Oberlin, Ohio, *not* the town of Bedrock. The family is always popping out in the (completely implausible) car to the drive-through restaurant for a slap-up meal of brontosaurus ribs, *even though* the first drive-through restaurant actually opened in 1948. In the Christmas episodes to which you object so strongly, the Flintstones are depicted enjoying the not-yet-applicable festival in an impossibly brightly lit cave decorated with balloons, *EVEN THOUGH* modern-style balloons were invented by Michael Faraday in 1824; and Fred, eschewing the hunter-gatherer career common to his contemporaries, takes a job as a department store Santa, **EVEN THOUGH** department stores were a nineteenth-century creation and St Nicholas, the original man behind the Santa beard, wasn't *born* until the year AD 270! Track down Hanna-Barbera and have them posthumously charged with fraud, because *The Flintstones* is a TISSUE OF LIES!

Troy Sexhammer: 'There's an old man sitting next to me/Makin' love to his tonic and gin . . .' Answer me this – how did Billy Joel manage to concentrate on knocking out a ballad with that going on in his peripheral vision?

Because Billy Joel is a pro, Mr Sexhammer (if that is your real name). He's not going to be distracted by someone using their penis as a swizzlestick when he's got work to do; when inspiration strikes, he is oblivious to all distractions. Rumour has it he finessed 'River of Dreams' at an Amsterdam sex show while a midget post-op transsexual fired pickled onions out of her parts.

Moz from Milton Keynes: Why are GMTV's competition questions so easy? Is it some sort of public service requirement to let stupid people win money? Or are they actually really difficult for the average GMTV viewer to answer? Is it ironic?

If the questions were as easy as you suggest, the competitions would be classed as unregulated lotteries, and Ofcom would be forced to fine the network. But GMTV is a bastion of responsibility and in no way sails close to the wind when it comes to such strict guidelines. That's why they make it so abundantly clear that you don't have to call the ENORMOUS, FLASHING PREMIUM RATE NUMBER on your screen to enter, but can also enter for free by visiting www.gm.tv.

Sadly for you, your cynicism has held you back from numerous fantastic opportunities to 'holiday like a soap star'. It's not too late for our other readers, though. Master the techniques of GMTV competition-answering and you too could bag yourself a TOP PRIZE. To help you hone your skills, here are some sample questions we have reprinted with permission from 'GMTV Brain Training'. Careful not to overexert yourself.

1 Who is the main character in William Shakespeare's play *Hamlet*?

    a) Hamlet

    b) King Rollo

    c) Harold Bishop

2 What is the traditional British accompaniment to battered fish?

    a) Chips

    b) Matzo balls

    c) Heartburn

3 Complete the title of this classic film: *Snow White and the Seven* ____

    a) Deadly Sins

    b) Dwarfs

    d) Gloryholes

4 Which of the following is not one of Queen Elizabeth's children?

    a) Prince Charles

    b) Princess Anne

    c) Noddy

5 Where is champagne from?

    a) France

    b) Egypt

    c) Oddbins

Remember to ask the permission of the person who pays the phone bill before calling in.

Tim from Watford: Why, at movie premieres, do stars walk down a red carpet?

In ancient times, red carpets were regarded as a luxury only fit for the Gods. Even Agamemnon, heading home from some top-class killing in Troy, was said to be too sheepish to walk 'a crimson path' – and he didn't have to talk to Ryan Seacrest about what he was wearing. But in the early twentieth century, the New York Central Railroad used red carpets to direct their clients towards the first-class cabins, inspiring the phrase 'red-carpet treatment', and ever since they've been a staple at fancy events like movie premieres.

Incidentally, stars don't really *walk* down the carpet: they dawdle, they pose, they pirouette, yapping to broadcast journalists and fraternising with fans along the way. Some find this latter act remarkable and seem to think they are somehow noble for doing it. Not at all. For one thing, actors have enormous egos and are naturally attracted to a wall of weeping girls screaming out their names and proffering body parts to be autographed. Secondly, Hollywood contracts contain promotion clauses – they are being *paid*, a lot, to be there. Most importantly, the press are present, and actors want to look good.

But just because they're taking their time, that doesn't mean they're enjoying themselves. It's hard to hide their need for a top-up of booze/coke/pills for the full length of a red carpet, and equally hard to look sexy and cool and calm whilst assiduously avoiding all the gossip-mongering hacks who want to harass them about their religion or sexuality. Add to this the fact that most successful actors are about as smart as an Oxo cube, and that bright red carpet must be a godsend: a scarlet arrow pointing to the safety of a darkened room where they can watch their own gorgeous faces for two whole hours and not have to smile at anyone.

? *Annabel: Is Humpty Dumpty really an egg?*

'Humpty Dumpty' was drummed into our heads as children, yet until receiving this question from Annabel we had never really analysed this baffling rhyme. Unlike most children's tales, it doesn't even seem to have a clear moral – don't sit on walls? Don't expect the King's horses to put you back together again when they have neither medical training nor opposable thumbs? Similarly, we had never considered Mr Dumpty's ovine appearance to be the slightest bit odd, but now we come to think of it, we've never seen a fully-clothed egg sitting on top of a wall. Not one.

Perhaps his egginess was made more explicit in earlier versions of the ditty, now consigned to the dustbin of history. Like Sylvia Plath and Edward II, Humpty Dumpty is defined by his death; rhymes about his life leading up to the moment he so famously sat on the wall must have faded into obscurity because they were so boring. Oral tradition isn't going to bother preserving:

> *Humpty Dumpty went to the shops,*
> *Humpty Dumpty bought some lamb chops,*
> *And then he went to the Day Centre for Eggs*
> *To take tea with his eggy friends.*

Or maybe his depiction as an egg arose as a more palatable alternative to this ugly rumour: that the original rhyme was based on a fourteenth-century Romanian prince who suffered from brittle bone syndrome and died after falling off his castle's battlements. Because kiddies should learn from an early age that incurable ailments and tragic death are the stuff of funny rhymes!

The fact is that 'Humpty Dumpty' is an example of a currently unfashionable entertainment genre: the riddle. I.e.: what would be irreparably broken if it fell off a wall? Answer (ignoring such secondary factors as why the King's entire military power would

That's Entertainment!

devote itself to mending it, or what it was doing atop a wall in the first place): an egg. Deprived of television and violent video-games, children of generations past considered deciphering such nonsensical imagery to be Fun; but now we all have access to real entertainment, like ringtones and Rick-rolling, riddles are not as popular as they used to be. So here's our foolproof version of 'Humpty Dumpty' for the stolidly literal-minded twenty-first-century child:

> *Humpty Dumpty looks like an egg,*
> *Humpty Dumpty smells of egg,*
> *Humpty Dumpty has a yolk and a white,*
> *Because Humpty Dumpty is an egg.*

No confusion there.

Kim from Edmonton, Alberta: *Have you ever played Ultimate Fris-bee? I would have thought such a sport would be right up your alley (no referees, relaxed, and a game designed by hippies).*

Sorry to disappoint you, Kim – and no doubt the Ultimate Frisbee Federation – but no, neither of us has ever played this so-called sport, which like all sports is but a game with the fun taken out.

You're right that we find it more appealing than other sports (shiny plastic! Pretty colours!), but that's no more an indication of enthusiasm than if we said we would rather have a lethal injection than allow an entire battalion to straddle our chests and shit in our mouths until we suffocate.

Furthermore, despite its origins as a toy for children and pets, Ultimate Frisbee also appears far too physically demanding for our liking: it requires lots of running, jumping, throwing, catching, hand-eye coordination and other such skills which have eluded us since birth. Helen's chances of triumphing in track and field are roughly equal to those of a Spelling Bee being won by an actual bee,* while Olly was once outrun by a deckchair in the 400 m relay.

James from the Philippines: What the hell is wrong with Wile E. Coyote? He always gets shit from ACME and it never works!

Wile E. Coyote is certainly a fool unto himself to keep throwing good money after bad. But it turns out Acme has got a fantastic loyalty card scheme. If Mr Coyote buys another three TNT detonators by the end of the year, he gets a free facial at Clarins!

Jacquelyne: Is it weird that I find myself sexually attracted to Anthony Hopkins as Dr Hannibal Lecter? I'm sure I'm not the only one.

What did it for you, Jacquelyne – the hammy acting? The hockey mask? The way he chewed that policeman's face off? Yes, it IS weird, you massive weirdo!

OUR TOP 5 WEIRD CRUSHES

OLLY
1 Janice from the Muppets
2 Gloria Hunniford
3 French finance minister Christine Lagarde
4 Diane Abbott
5 Jared Leto

HELEN
1 Inspector Morse
2 Will Arnett
3 Dr Cox from *Scrubs*
4 Bette Davis
5 Tim Gunn

* Except for when playing 'fetch' with her family dog, at which point she becomes a champion athlete.

Robert from Dumfriesshire: What is it exactly that Meat Loaf won't do for love?

We assume Robert is referring to Meat Loaf's 1993 mega-hit 'I'd Do Anything For Love (But I Won't Do That)', and doesn't expect us to go interrogating Mr Loaf's exes or rifling through his bins in search of an answer. Analysing the lyrics doesn't help, as they provide an embarrassment of riches: Meat won't ever lie to you, or forget the way you feel right now, or stop dreaming of you every night of his life. More creepily, he will also never forgive himself if you don't go all the way tonight – but at least he promises never to do it better than he does it with you. His most adamant promise, passionately declared towards the song's conclusion, is that he won't screw around.

Gallant though these ambitions are, none seem exciting enough to justify being the 'THAT' in one of the most long-winded artistic works in human history. So let's have a look at the clues left in the video, directed by Michael '*Pearl Harbor* and other shit films' Bay, to see what Meat is *really* not doing for love. Why don't you watch along with us?

0 mins 07 secs: A fleet of police cars and a helicopter pursue a man on a motorcycle. Could it be Mr Loaf? Perhaps he is wanted for murder, tax evasion, or riding a bike with a broken light. We are pleased to note he is wearing a helmet; one thing he *won't* do for love is compromise road safety.

0 mins 37 secs: The man rides into a gothic cemetery swathed in dry ice. Will he be able to shake off the rozzers in there? The vocal kicks in, and – hey, wait a minute! The man on the bike can't be Meat Loaf himself, because he is watching the events from a hedge! He is sporting foul inch-long fingernails. You might think he'd take his eye out with those; but he won't do that.

1 min 20 secs: Police enter a shadowy catacomb, carrying massive guns and shining their torches at the chandelier, even though there's no way tubby old Meat could be hiding in it. It's in dire need of a good dusting, but Meat won't do that, not with his allergies.

1 min 38 secs: The motorcycle bursts through the wall! Guns are fired, policemen scatter, chandeliers fall to the floor. A hand lies lifeless. Meat's landlord will never give him his deposit back now.

1 min 55 secs: Oh no! A sexy lady in a giant birdbath spots Meat perving on her from the trees. He drops a piece of costume jewellery he shoplifted from Claire's Accessories, and legs it. Sexy lady follows, because returning lost property is a noble thing to do.

2 mins 41 secs: Ooh, that's better – Meat takes a break in his chair by the fire in his big gothic mansion, enjoying a goblet of Bovril. The sexy lady's face seems to swim across the drink's surface, but that's probably just scum because Meat lives in a hardwater area.

3 mins 23 secs: The sexy lady enters the house and Meat's chair suddenly shoots off to one side, a bit like when people are bored at the office and dicking around on their swivel chairs. His refusal to lay carpets for love is really paying off now – wheeeeee!

3 mins 41 secs: Meat catches sight of himself in an ornate mirror. Ooh, he's ugly! The sexy lady, all mucky from the woods and Meat's filthy house, decides to have a bath. The water must be freezing, because Meat seems to subscribe to the notion that four dozen candelabras in each room is a viable substitute for a combi boiler.

4 mins 02 secs: Police tape seals off the catacomb, as the fuzz sift through splinters of chandelier and dead officer. A man who closely resembles Niles from Frasier looks really pissed off. Meat is in *so* much trouble!

4 mins 12 secs: A close-up shot of a pupil dilating. This is to mark the video's halfway point. Only another six hours to go.

4 mins 16 secs: Not content with breaking into a stranger's house and taking a bath, the sexy lady is now writhing around in Meat's bed. We've read *Goldilocks and the Three Bears*, and this isn't going to end well. Suddenly, some of her sexy nymph friends appear and lez her up! But Meat has turned his back on this saucy scene. You would think he might watch and fondle his Man Meat, but he won't do that because he disapproves of homosexuality.

5 mins 12 secs: Meat smashes a mirror with a stick. Don't do that, Meat – it's seven years' bad luck!

5 mins 42 secs: As if Sexy Lady wasn't finding Meat Loaf's house weird enough, the chaise longue she's reclining on suddenly rises ten feet in the air. Like many men, Meat Loaf refused to ask help when assembling his flatpack furniture, and has been ruing his foolish pride ever since.

5 mins 51 secs: Boobs akimbo, the sexy lady begins to sing as police swarm the house. The candles blow out and, in the darkness, Meat and the lady finally meet. It's hard to tell which of them is wearing more make-up. 'Sooner or later you'll be screwing around,' she emotes. 'I won't do that!' bawls Meat, knowing that with his leathery face, chance would be a fine thing.

7 mins 08 secs: A beam of sunlight hits Meat right in the eye, and suddenly his fake fingernails, gothy make-up and strange forehead-ridges disappear, leaving in their place . . . Meat Loaf's face. Hey, isn't that the guy from *Spice World*? No matter: he and the lady vanish, reappearing on a motorbike riding into the sunrise. Try catching them now, police – you won't do that!

After that thorough investigation, we therefore surmise that Meat Loaf won't do the following for love:

1 Keep his house neat and tidy
2 Use electricity
3 Look at a mirror without smashing it.

George from Aberdeenshire: If Britain's 'Got Talent', what have other countries got?

More impressive native cuisine, and better weather.

Billy from Featherstone: In your opinion, what is the greatest weapon of all time in any video game?

In all honesty, our experience of the medium is too slight for our opinions to be truly valuable. Helen's childhood console, the Amstrad CPC464, took so long to load a shoot-'em-up that it would have been quicker to hammer out a UN Resolution than fire a bullet, whilst Olly's preferred puzzle-and-platform titles on his Amiga 500 were so luridly happy-clappy that even Barney the Dinosaur would consider them light on violence.

Nonetheless, we recall some excellent, albeit leftfield, pixelated weaponry in the games that we did play. In *PaperBoy*, a tame precursor of *Grand Theft Auto*, you inhabit the body of a suburban adolescent with a minimum-wage job (yay escapism!), whose principal weapon was . . . rolled-up newspapers. These you could chuck at various provincial targets on your delivery round, including a church window and the adjacent graveyard. Pow! You just cracked a tombstone in half. Splat! You've crashed into a fat man out for a jog. Crunch! You've fallen off your bike, because you tried to kill a dog. This game won't allow you to do that, because killing animals is wrong. Go desecrate some more cemeteries, kid.

But our vote for the greatest videogame weapon of all time is also the most innocuous: the day-glo rainbows wielded by the babyfaced protagonist of classic arcade game *Rainbow Islands: The Story of Bubble Bobble 2*. With sinister enthusiasm this sick little prick strewed about noxious multicoloured explosions, bringing death and destruction to all around him as he merrily hopped around an island that was slowly sinking into the sea thanks to the nuclear winter he was leaving in his wake. So intense was the afterglow of these bursts of light that cute little insects were immediately incinerated and turned into WATERMELONS. Which he then ATE. And all to the tune of a MIDI interpretation of 'Somewhere Over The Rainbow'. That beats any of those flame-throwing, machine-gunny surrogate schlongs used to pulverise baddies in modern-day gorefests, hands down.

Olly says:

To the delicate young Olly Mann, the most petrifying computerised weapon was not used by me, but against me: the killer tadpoles spat out by the scary Monster Octopus at the end of the 'Sea of Karnaugh' level in the space game *Menace*. This represented a fearsome challenge, so to prepare ourselves for each afternoon's gaming, I used to act it out in the ▶

Answer Me This!

45

playground with my childhood friend Oliver Sloboda. For some reason, I always had to play the humble rocket ship, and Oliver Sloboda the Monster Octopus, who spat repeatedly in my face like an anti-Semite from the 1930s. ∎

Helen says:

When you have to sit in the coldest room of a cold house for up to half an hour waiting for your game cassette to load, you are bloody well determined to enjoy whatever game whirrs into life. Thus my pleasure did not discriminate between *Harrier Attack* (Falklands War-inspired bombing game), *Monty Python* (you play Mr Gumby, hopping around on a boot eating sausages), *Kane* (cowboy kills birds), or even the *Spitting Image* Amstrad game, in which 1980s world leaders were pitted against each other in a series of duels, using the greatest weapon of all: their bare hands. Kapow! That's the sound of Mikhail Gorbachev knocking seven bells out of P. W. Botha! Did the nine-year-old me know who P. W. Botha was? Of course not! Computer violence is always the victor in the bareknuckle duel with out-of-date political satire.

Matt from Barnehurst: Why do cartoons always represent drunk people with hiccups? I've been drunk loads of times and never hiccupped at all!

Think how animators represent sexual attraction: with the character's heart pulsating out of their chest. This symbolic shortcut is felt to be more appropriate for a family audience than depicting a massive boner. Similarly, when a character bangs their head, tweeting birdies circle above, even though a more realistic representation would include a rush to Intensive Care, a two-week coma, and permanent brain damage.

It's mildly amusing to see Donald Duck hiccupping as he takes a swig from the wrong bottle and bumps into a tree; it's less comical to see him crash an office party, grope some ducks who aren't Daisy, and spew up all over himself after glassing Mickey for waving at him.

Matt from Barnehurst, meanwhile, should count himself lucky – other people definitely suffer from drunken hiccups, including Olly's girlfriend, who likes to try to cure them by phoning him late at night and ranting about London Underground.

Mike in Cape Town: I heard Mariah Carey say her eleventh album was called E=MC^2 *because it stood for 'Emancipation = Mariah Carey x 2'* (The Emancipation of Mimi *being her previous album*). *What was hilarious was that she thought that to square something was the same as multiplying by two. It seems to me that in the celebrity world, being stupid is an asset. Why?*

Singers and actors only become mega-celebs if their private lives get as much press attention as their careers. And the private lives of unintelligent people are more headline-grabbing than those of brainboxes, because they make more mistakes: marrying evil bounders, getting indoctrinated by money-grabbing cults, shaving off their eyebrows, flashing their privates whilst getting out of cars, jerking off in public toilets, buying expensive houses on the waterfront despite the rising sea levels. So, those performers who fall out of the stupid tree and hit every branch on the way down are more likely to rise to the top of the tabloid agenda.

The more attention these dolts receive, the more bankable they become; so, irrespective of critically panned albums and movies, they are rewarded for their dimwittedness with book deals, perfume ranges and million-dollar advertising contracts. They then tend to become romantically involved with fellow thick celebrities to beef up their column inches, knowing they'll get even more money and tabloid exposure if they manage to spawn together. So, over time, the celebrity gene pool will degrade into utter gormlessness, until we will all be able to spot a celebrity child on the street by their massive beard, crumpled trousers, and habit of swatting invisible flies with their hands. Intelligent celebrities should do the decent thing and prevent this decline. We therefore call on Stephen Fry to start procreating with Cate Blanchett as soon as is mutually convenient.

Holly in Brockley: Why is it bad luck to say 'Macbeth' in the theatre, and where does this tradition come from?

Let's point the finger of blame, like a big, blood-drenched sword, squarely at the source: ACTORS.

Think on it, Holly. Actors are very imaginative. They spend their time pretending to be other people, which after a while is bound to bend the mind. Plus, they work in an industry which does not encourage common sense, whilst at the same time allowing them far too much spare time in which to spread superstition and propagate conspiracies. If you're whiling away the whole day waiting to go on and say three lines at the end of Act Two, you need a hobby: driving your colleagues into a tizzy about rabbits' feet, white heather and The Scottish Play is cheap, portable and endless fun.

No, the most sensible explanation we've come across is the following: because *Macbeth* was a big blockbuster in its day, struggling theatre companies would often mount a production of it in an attempt to turn their fortunes around. But, since they were on their last legs anyway, the production was usually their final curtain. Hence the play, through no especial fault of its own, became known as a curse on theatre companies.

Not content with this logic, some prefer to lay the blame upon Shakespeare himself, gibbering that he cursed the play by incorporating real witches' spells in the text. Do us a favour: if he'd known how to craft an effective spell, he would have vaporised all folios of *The Two Noble Kinsmen*.

Olly says:

I have first-hand experience of The Scottish Play's sinister powers. At the age of eight, I played Son of Macduff in a fringe production, which was pretty good fun, because I got stabbed to death each night with a retractable blade. Except, one night, the blade didn't retract, and although I was somehow spared, Mrs Macduff was stabbed right in the stomach.

Ever the professional, the injured actress continued with the scene, which wasn't too difficult because she was only required to drop down dead. When the lights went down she was whisked off to A&E, and thankfully made a full recovery. Unfortunately, she was playing more than one role in the production, so attentive members of the audience did observe that only two out of the three witches returned for the final scene.

Oli: *If Nintendo is a Japanese company then why is its star character Mario supposed to be Italian?*

If your logic had prevailed and one could only create characters who share one's own nationality, cultural tragedy would result. There never would have been *'Allo 'Allo* or Manuel from *Fawlty Towers*, while *Romeo and Juliet* would have been considerably less poignant had the leads been called Ron and Julie. And where would the Bond franchise be without ludicrous Eastern European villains?

We doubt that when Mario's creator, Shigero Miyamoto, was coming up with the dungaree-sporting plumber, his thought process ran anything like this: 'OK, he lives in Mushroom Kingdom, and there's a giant snail for him to ride around on. So far, so realistic. But hold on – nobody's going to believe this guy's *Japanese*! What Japanese man would sport such a big bushy moustache, anyway? Better make him Italian. I hear anything goes over there.' Nay. Mario – who started his career in the sewers of New York, which Oli here probably thinks is a bit off as well – was originally going to be called Jumpman or Mr Video. Lameissimo! Then one fateful day, the landlord of the Nintendo mothership, a Seattle property magnate called Mario Segale, came round to scream at Mr Miyamoto and his fellow Nintendites, who had fallen behind in their rent. To appease him, they decided to name their character 'Mario', just as we will be calling the hero of our debut novel 'Foxtons Lettings' so that we don't get evicted.

Acatia from Bar Hill: *Are there actually any rules for Eurovision?*

Yes! It might look like a sparkly vision of bedlam with a double portion of extra cheese, but there are in fact rigid rules. The Ten Commandments of Eurovision are:

1 Contestants must wave and smile at the camera at least once during their performance, whether their song is a singalong disco spectacular or a mournful ballad about the war tearing apart their homeland.

2 All hairstyles must be inspired by the original 1984 production of *Starlight Express*.

3 All men must resemble either Ian McShane or H from Steps, but never both.

4 Five points will be deducted from any song not containing the lyrics 'la la la', 'yeah yeah yeah', or 'Tora! Tora! Tora!'

5 Israel is in Europe.

6 Palestine is not in Europe.

7 The hosts of the award – one male, one female – must be not up to the job in any way.

8 The videos promoting the host country between each act must contain the following images:
   – a couple walking hand-in-hand by a fruit market
   – some old men playing chess in the sunshine
   – a little girl spinning around in a white lace dress
   – a crane shot of a bell tower
   – some ladies with nice boobs smiling as if caught off-guard.

9 All countries must give their highest score to their closest neighbours, except for France and Ireland, who will snub their good friends Great Britain.

10 Extra points will be added for dance routines involving clapping, twirling, or removal of clothes. If all three are achieved at once, this will be considered the greatest cultural feat of all time.

Damian from South Wales: *Who the fuck do the presenters of Top Gear think they are?*

They all think they are Jeremy Clarkson.

Vile Bodies

Is it normal to have hair there? Does anyone else have funny-looking —s? Is that odour natural? Hahahahaha, OF COURSE NOT! But even freaks like you might find solace in this section, as we take a whistlestop tour from cerebellum to perineum and, um, back again.

Laura: Why are supermarket own-brand wet wipes called 'baby wipes' when most of the people using them aren't babies?

Because 'baby wipes' sounds a lot more innocent than 'removing your smudged make-up after a one-night-stand wipes' or 'cleaning your armpits at a music festival wipes'. Smoke-and-mirrors, Laura, smoke-and-mirrors.

Fiona from County Durham: If a corpse has been dug up after being underground for about a month, and you chopped it into bits, would it bleed?

That seems a weirdly specific question, Fiona. Let's not dwell on why you've asked it, as by the time this book is published, justice should have caught up with you. Anyway, the entirely hypothetical corpse of which you speak would not bleed, no;* blood

***

* Although we'd still recommend that you remove your best tablecloth before plonking a recently-exhumed body on your dining table.

congeals pretty quickly without a living heart pumping it round the body, which is how we get scabs and black pudding. It is wise not to think of the connection between those things when you're trying to enjoy a Full English.

Tom from Colyton: What is the best way to get a tan without increasing the chance of getting skin cancer?

Take a tip from ladies painting on trompe-l'oeil stockings during World War II and smear yourself with gravy browning. It will give you a deep melanoma-free tan, as well as a rich beefy aroma.

Olly says:

You know those weird salesmen who march along the beach, flogging baskets of shite no one wants? My dad once bought some suntan lotion from one of them. Insane, but not out of character: Dad regularly traipses round Selfridges for hours without finding a single thing to buy, yet after ten minutes soaking up the sun is enchanted by knock-off sunglasses, souvenir T-shirts and hats made from banana skins.

So he hands over a fiver for this unlabelled brown bottle of sticky yellow liquid that looks like something out of *George's Marvellous Medicine*, and liberally douses his entire torso and legs with it (doing a patch test of this unsealed, unlicensed product would, of course, be a total waste of time, what with his busy holiday schedule of sitting on a beach all day doing dick-all). Fifteen minutes goes by, and he's ▶

Vile Bodies

half-asleep, half-reading his back issue of *Classic & Sports Car*, and then he asks me, 'Can you smell . . . burning?'

There are no barbecues on this particular beach, and no chimneys either. Suddenly suspicious of his recent purchase, Dad dabs a blob of the 'lotion' on his finger and licks it. Sunflower oil. He runs into the sea to wash himself off before he becomes crispy. Mum and I laugh, a lot. ∎

Seb from Brighton: Why is it that my twin brother has a significantly bigger wanger than I do?

If only Seb had seen the DeVito–Schwarzenegger vehicle *Twins*, he would know that it is not at all unusual for twins to differ physically – especially if they were created in a screwball Aryan eugenics experiment.

The disparity may be mere illusion, courtesy of perspective. Since Seb is looking down at his own little mollusc from above, rather than admiring its statuesque beauty from the head-on viewpoint from which he has been sinisterly studying his brother's Todgersaurus Rex, it could be that his own merely *appears* to be smaller, when in fact it is of comparable size. Male readers will be familiar with this concept from every teen advice column or sexual health website they have ever accidentally stumbled upon whilst searching for jack-off material.

Possible comforts aside, let's face it: Seb could be right. Moreover he might be possessed of not only a much smaller cock than his brother, but actually a teeny-weeny conker-cock. No point encouraging him to look at it from a different angle. A micropenis will always be a micropenis, even if he jams the ruler deep into his abdominal wall and deliberately misreads millimetres as inches.

?

But if this is indeed the case, Seb, so what? No one is likely ever to witness your two appendages side-by-side to make the comparison, unless you share a girlfriend, your mum happens to walk in as you're both getting changed after swimming, or you both plan a career in pornography.

Samantha: Why does 'fanny' mean a lady's front bottom when it used to be a woman's name?

Yes, pity the poor woman whose parents insisted on giving her the old-fashioned abbreviation of Frances as a nickname! Maybe she could move to the US, where 'fanny' is slang for a person's back bottom – still not ideal, but a slight improvement.

Fanny-as-in-a-lady lent itself to fanny-as-in-ladybits thanks to John Cleland, author of the sauciest bonkbuster of 1748, *Fanny Hill*. Though nowadays it is a breezeblock-sized set text that English literature students snooze through, at the time the novel was so unprecedentedly racy that it was banned before it corrupted every literate man and woman in the empire. Ladies' unmentionables became named after the libidinous titular heroine, because she was officially the first woman in British history to have genitals.

Lucas from Berlin: You know if you smoke a bit of pot, and then you're well hungry, why are you well hungry? I've always spent all my money on the pot, so can't afford anything to eat!

Dude, we haven't got the foggiest idea what you're yabbing about. We wouldn't . . . er, why would you think . . . Why are you *looking* at us? What have we *done*? Oh, man – there's a cat on the chair! That's so fucked up! Hahahahahahaha.

Anyway. The hunger you're experiencing comes courtesy of

the cannabinoids in the drug, which trigger your brain's cannabinoid receptors. Pay attention, you can watch some *Spongebob Squarepants* in a minute. These receptors are activated when you're born, and it's due to them that babies feel hunger, and sup at mummy's teat, even if at the time they aren't really into boobies. That's right, boobies! Funny.

Once you grow older, and eating becomes part of your daily routine, your receptors are supposed to lie low and, you know, *chill out* – but then when you have a toke, they get stimulated and as a result you feel hungry. We're not sure why it is that they tell your brain to eat four Big Macs and a Snickers bar rather than suckle on a nipple for sustenance, but it's in everyone's best interests that they do.

Louisa: Do bald men wash their hair with soap or shampoo?

Helen asked her slaphead dad this question, and he very firmly said, 'Shampoo.' He still has his pride, goddammit.

Katherine: Why are period pains sooooooooooo painfuuuuuuuullll?

To remind you and all women of the wickedness of their fruit-beguiled forebear Eve. And to prop up the hot-water bottle industry.

Barbara from Dumfriesshire: What causes ladies of a certain age to suddenly start sprouting awful thick hairs – especially white ones which are a bugger to pluck out? I am told it is stress, and hormones (too many, too few). I am a victim of this awful 'disease' and have tried everything from plucking to bleaching, buffing and electrolysis; but, at last, the most costly cure of all has hit me! LASER!! To get all my fuzz orf my face will cost me around a grand; please reassure me that this treatment will be worth it – I just feel so bloody guilty at spending such a fortune.

Laser – but of course! We've all sat watching *Star Trek* and thought, those phasers certainly seem effective at incinerating enemy star-ships: let's try them on our stubble. But Barbara, the sad truth is that, despite laser-wielders' claims that they can rid you of your ladytache permanently, your face might only be temporarily fuzz-free: fast-forward a decade and you could possess a white beard as thick and bushy as jolly old St Nick's. So, no, it's not worth a thousand pounds: for a tenth of that price you could buy yourself a decent Flymo and do a better job yourself.

As for why these hairs have arrived: yes, those turbulent hor-mones are making their presence known via your facial follicles. Tempting though it must be, we wouldn't recommend you at-tempt to rebalance this by topping up your oestrogen without medical supervision, unless you want a tit growing out of your neck or something. Just remind yourself that beneath your coat of fur, you're still the nubile sex muppet you always were, and that there are plenty of people out there prepared to pay good money to peek at pictures of hairy women. Cut up some old carpet tiles, stick them to your every orifice and satisfy that niche market in-stead: not only will you save your £1000, you could actually end up making money!

Jim in New Jersey: I once had some pretentious would-be Boho neighbours who planted their child's placenta under a fig tree in their front yard. Appallingly, they invited friends and neighbours to the 'ceremony', and even more appallingly, several people actually attended. (I saw it all from my window, cringing.) Do you know where and how this nonsense got started?

Placenta-planting has reared its weirdy head with remarkable regularity throughout history, and continues to be a hallowed custom in some patches of the globe. Some tribes consider the placenta to be part of the baby and therefore want to dispose of it with respect; others fear the parents' future fertility might be damaged by the proximity of the spooky afterbirth if it remains above ground.

Though they might find us just as odd for consigning placentas to the hospital incinerator, our favourite placenta-disposers are the Kwakiutl tribe of Canada. They bury the placentas of their newborn daughters to ensure they grow up to be expert at digging clams, and feed those of their sons to ravens to encourage future prophetic visions. Here's a vision for you, Kwakiutl: send your kids to clam-digging college instead, you'll get better results.

At least Jim's neighbours didn't get involved in placentophagy, the craze (in both senses of the word) of eating your baby's placenta. We're not parents ourselves, but if that's the kind of thing you consider when you have a child, sterilise us tomorrow. Surely, in a world which doesn't turn its nose up at black puddings, chopped liver and peperami, if placentas were actually tasty, they'd be part of our regular diet. There would be Kentucky Fried Placenta, Sainsbury's Taste the Difference organic placentas, and Delia's Placenta Crumble with Placenta Custard. But there aren't, and all the placenta recipes we've ever seen involve copious quantities of fried onion, garlic and spices to disguise the flavour of the star ingredient. As for the superstition that eating your newborn's placenta might ward off post-natal depression: eating their poo would provide a diversion from inner torment too, but it wouldn't address the root causes.

Stop playing coy, Amelia: you only went and got yourself a hickey because you wanted a visible sign that you're getting some action. Since you've already gone to the trouble, you might as well emphasise it with a massive arrow-shaped earring and a coating of glitter.

Helen says:

Blimey, it's a long time since I saw a hickey! That's because I am thirty years old and not sixteen. But even as a teen, I was quite revolted by the trend, and poured scorn upon the girls who used purple eyeshadow, vicious pinching or even the hoover nozzle to create an imitation blood-bruise upon their unfortunate neck-flesh.

Here's how the young me would have disguised the gruesome ornamentation, had Common Sense (and a boyfriend who was averse to deliberate blood-drawing) not alleviated me of the problem.

Helen's Top 5 Hickey-Hiders

1 neck brace, pretending I'd been in a minor car accident
2 Elizabethan ruff
3 bee-keeper's head-dress
4 nun's wimple
5 stick-on Santa beard

Rob from Portsmouth: I was driving along the other day, having just picked up my lovely boyfriend Nathan from work, when he asked if he could lick me (I am not keen on being licked so he does it to annoy me). I said 'NO'. He then asked when it would be an appropriate time to lick me and I replied, 'When I am dead.' He said that his taste buds would not be working when I am dead, they would be worn out and he wouldn't be able to taste anything. So answer me this: do taste buds wear out when you're old?

How commendable that, despite your boyfriend's blatant perversions, you are thinking long-term about this relationship. If you and Nathan remain together until you are old and grey and then you pass away, Nathan would be so consumed with grief that whipping out his withered geriatric tongue for a final lick of your cold dead flesh would be the last thing on his mind. YOU WIN! However, if he did remember the oath you made all those decades ago, he would discover that, like all human cells, taste buds do indeed die off as you get older. He might not taste anything at all. But his oral disappointment would be tempered by being proved victorious in your car argument at last.

Donna Prima: Today in drama class we had to do a performance which was being recorded. I was wearing a quite low-cut vest top and had to bend down, unknowingly showing the rest of the class my boobs. The person I have a crush on is also in my drama group and saw the whole thing, and now we have to watch it back and it's also being shown to the year above. So answer me this: how do I talk to him (or anyone else in my drama group for that matter) and watch the video without being completely embarrassed?

We fail to see the problem here. Teenage boys like boobs. You have shown your boobs. This will not work against you, we promise.

Georgina from Surrey: Why was I subjected to watching Loose Women *at the dentist? Surely dental TV should make you feel better about being there!*

After fifteen minutes of that, we bet your root canal didn't feel half as painful, did it?

Andrew from the Wirral: Is it appropriate to put deodorant around your genitals?

It would be more appropriate to have a shower occasionally, Captain Stinkyballs.

Joss: What do you do if you wet yourself on a train?

Deflect attention from the piss on your trousers by taking a dump on someone in First Class.

Peter in Livingston: Why do you need to brush your teeth in the morning when you ate nothing all night?

Back away Pete, your breath stinks! Look, if some tooth-obsessed loon puts a gun to your head and insists that you only brush once a day for the rest of your life, then you're right, it would be more sensible to opt for brushing at night than in the morning. There's a day's worth of food detritus clinging to your enamels by bedtime, and you don't want to allow it to frolic in your mouth for a further eight hours. However, gun-toting weirdoes aside, it's pretty obvious that brushing twice a day is twice as good for you as brushing once; and don't forget that overnight bacteria gather on your teeth which, if left to accumulate, will give you molten fangs and breath fit to melt diamonds. Now please go and freshen up.

Olly says:

One night at boarding school I squeezed out bits of everyone's toothpaste into a large tub. I realise this sounds like the opening stages of a sinister wanking game, but it was actually one of my earliest entrepreneurial exercises.

I added some extra ingredients: chunks of chewing gum for flavour, a dash of apple juice for colour, and a squirt of Listerine for fresh breath. I hung a poster in the common room claiming I had invented a new type of toothpaste, and with all the chutzpah of an 11-year-old Jew, proceeded to sell samples of it to my cohorts at a significant mark-up.

100 per cent of my 'customers' loved it – although at the time most of them also loved Color Me Badd, so in retrospect their patronage was easily won. The outlandish success of this experiment (gross profit: £0.75) might even have been repeated across subsequent evenings, but sadly my miracle mixture, unprotected from the elements, soon hardened into a grey grout. My dreams of becoming the youngest toothpaste magnate in the Home Counties ossified with it.

Kerry: Why does Barbie have such big boobs? They seem even more out of proportion than Lara Croft's! Why give her such big ones, when Ken has nothing down there . . . I'm not advocating doll porn, but a bit of equality surely?

Is it any wonder Ken's wang is a retracted mangina? He's been dating Barbie for more than fifty frustrating years. In all that time, flesh-coloured plastic underwear has been permanently affixed to his pelvis. *He's never even seen his own penis.* Meanwhile, his girlfriend's assets have been pumped up and deflated numerous times. Each time, Ken has waited patiently, hoping against hope that now – surely now, in the twenty-first century – he might finally be permitted to unleash the plastic dragon. But no. Barbie is the world's biggest ever cock-tease, with the world's most improbable proportions before or since Lolo Ferrari.

At the time of writing, Barbie's vital statistics, scaled up from doll size to real woman size, would result in D-cup boobs and an 18-inch waist. This physique is unobtainable to most women without recourse to surgery, anorexia, or clamping their stomachs in a vice. But here's the thing about adults: they don't play with Barbie dolls. And kids, in our experience, don't aspire to be like their playthings; not really. Olly's favourite toy was Mr Potato Head. Scaled up to human size, this freak of nature would possess a 92-inch waist, no genitals and a moustache as wide as his feet. But Olly didn't want to *be* Mr Potato Head; he knew he was just a character. The fact that Olly does now resemble him is mere coincidence.

Jack from Stoke: What are 'bingo wings'?

They are a much-missed component of KFC's discontinued Gambling Meal Deal, along with the Roulette Cobette and Poker Chips. We jest, we jest! Bingo wings are actually the flappy bits of flesh under the upper arms of elderly ladies, who remain the biggest bingo-playing demographic, despite the efforts of TV campaigns portraying thirtysomethings out for a shag-and-scratchcard.

When a lucky bingoist has filled her card, she leaps up in excitement shouting 'House!', at which point said bingo wings wobble with the excitement of victory. As bingo diminishes in popularity, the bingo wings of future generations of geriatrics will probably be renamed. Our money's on 'Wii wings'.

Jim from Sydney: What's the worst haircut you've ever had, and did it go away?

It went away, then it grew back again, then it went away, then it grew back again . . . We've had so many appalling haircuts it would be unfair to single out just one. It seems most hairdressers skip the curly-hair module at styling school; or else we can't account for why we, and all our frizzy-topped brethren, habitually suffer such abominations. Helen has involuntarily been given so many disastrous blunt bobs, scrunch dries, and fringes (a fringe? With curly hair? Laws ought to be passed) that she now resorts to cutting her hair herself; it is a safer system than pleading for clemency from the Darren or Sharon casually holding sharp blades millimetres from her vital blood vessels.

The biggest travesty wrought on Olly's head wasn't cut-related, but an accident of colour, and entirely self-inflicted. Inspired by one of his friends, who at the time had enviable Kurt Cobain-like surfy blond locks,* Olly rushed to Superdrug and stocked up on hair-lightening sun-spray. He liberally applied this bleachy lemon solution to his rodent-coloured Jewfro, took to the beach and readied himself to morph into *Troy*-era Brad Pitt.

His hair immediately lightened, to a kind of nondescript medium-brown. The next day, he applied twice as much, to speed up the process. Day Three, it went lighter still: orangey. And that. Is where. It stopped. Day Four, Day Five, Day Six: endless re-applications of the spray – Olly stinking of fake citrus, his scalp feeling like it was on fire – but his hair stubbornly remained as vibrantly tangerine as Julianne Moore's muff. Although film buffs were keen on it in Robert Altman's *Short Cuts*, they cer-

---

* He's now rapidly balding, Oliver 'Schadenfreude' Mann is pleased to report.

Answer Me This!

tainly didn't love it atop Olly's head. The ladies stayed away, and 'Surf-Style Olly' was put on permanent hiatus.

Lew in the Czech Republic: When the navy performs a burial at sea, do they weight the coffin so you sink to the bottom, or do they just leave you bobbing around on the surface?

It depends upon the religious faith of the shipmates. Some refuse to bury at sea at all, since an afterlife as a snack for plankton was not part of the Almighty's plan. Others cremate the body on board, and either accidentally-on-purpose knock the ashes over the side if they're in an area of international waters which frowns upon polluting the sea with burnt ground-up corpses, or bring them home to give to the bereaved family.

When they do decide to commit the late sailor's corpse to splashdown, they do tend to add weights to the coffin – or, rather, the sailcloth into which the body is sewn, there not being the room for a stack of coffins onboard busy ships. They also make an effort to throw the body into waters where there don't appear to be many predators around, because the last thing grieving sailors want to see is the shark-chewed body of Able-Seaman Timmy bobbing past on the crest of a blood-tinged wave.

Jonny: Are we all gonna die?

Yes. Except for David Attenborough, hopefully.

James from Gloucestershire: Do pink socks exist? Not the clothes, obviously: the myth that if you bum someone and then whack their head it makes their anal muscles tighten so much that if you whip your dick out it turns their bum inside out. I hope it's not true, because it's fucking grim.

Helen says:

Here's a sea-burial fact for you, readers, and whoever would have thought I might have one of those up my sleeve, eh? I was told it at the age of five when visiting Admiral Lord Nelson's ship, HMS *Victory*, on a family outing to Portsmouth. Take *that*, Olly, with all your childhood trips to Sea World.

What I learnt from the HMS *Victory* – and I wouldn't dare doubt it – is that when sailors died at sea, they were sewn into their hammocks and chucked off the side of the boat. But because in those days life at sea was hardly a P&O cruise around the Med, lots of sailors used to pretend to be dead, so that they would be despatched from the boat, whereupon they could cut themselves out of the hammock and swim a few hundred nautical miles to dry land.

Presumably smelling a rat after a rash of sudden deaths among seemingly healthy sailors, the ship's hammock-stitchers decided to employ a new tactic to make sure the body was properly dead: as they closed up the hammock, they would take care to sew right through the sailor's nose. Even methodical old De Niro would have struggled to play dead with a bodkin through the snout.

If that's what passes for a myth these days, we've never missed Zeus more.

Let's get one thing straight, James from Gloucestershire: though anxious not to renege on our question-answering duties, we are not willing to submit ourselves to a practical experiment to prove whether or not pink socks work. You will just have to content yourself with our theoretical reasons for believing this to be but fiction, fiction so repulsive that the whole human race should wash their mouths out with carbolic soap to repent for the fact that someone, somewhere dreamt it up.

Firstly, we don't think that thumping someone in the head would make any part of their innards clench – probably they would have the opposite reaction. Secondly, in our VERY tentative internet research, we found the putative practice to be illustrated by photos of saucy naked ladies on all fours with what looked like a glossy pink legwarmer protruding from their posteriors. We believe these pictures to be fakes. Why? Because in the event that our digestive systems fall out of our arses, we would be hobbling to the hospital as fast as possible, without pausing for a moment to take provocative pictures of ourselves.

Solids and Liquids

When we're not using our mouths to answer questions or blow kisses at kittens, we like to use them to scoff things. It's not an uncommon pursuit. If you don't want to know how much fat is in your milkshake or where sausages come from, keep your eyes closed whilst reading this section.

Josh: Why do people care what shape pasta they eat? I don't.

We suspect you *would* care, Josh, if you were served up a plate-ful of swastika carbonara. But there's no arguing that pasta is the same damn dough whichever way you twist it, from angel-hair to ziti. As an Alphabetti-munching idiot Brit, you'll surely never fully appreciate the subtle distinctions between fettucine and tagliatelle; but on pasta's home turf, bloody battles have been fought over such matters.

You see, Italians are highly particular about matching the shape of pasta to the appropriate sauce, and if you innocently presented them with a piping-hot bowlful of fusilli alla vongole or linguine al forno, they might slap you in the face and then reverse over you with their Vespa. Even though we can't even tell our strangolapreti from our sacchettoni, we do understand the basic principle that a fine clingy sauce suits thin, stringy pasta, and a thicker, lumpier sauce needs a more robust pasta counterpart. To this end – and don't blow a gasket when you read this, Josh – the Italians have come up with a whopping 350 different types of pasta shapes. Excessive? Well, at least it presents myriad extra possibilities for kindergarten pasta collages.

Given how seriously those Italians take pasta, we can only imagine how much distress foreign perversions of their favourite carbohydrate must cause them. '*Dio mio!*' they cry at the sight of novelty penis-and-boobs pasta in Ann Summers, and cartons of tuna and sweetcorn pasta salad in Boots. If any of them ever happen upon the Durham restaurant in which Helen spotted spaghetti bolognese served *on top of a pizza*, run down to the cellar with six weeks' water and supplies, because the fallout could be the end of us all.

Lesley-Anne from the side of the road: Do fish have livers? Cos of cod liver oil . . .

You've answered your own question, Lesley-Anne. Look again closely. Cod liver oil. *Cod* LIVER *oil*. Do you still not see it? **LIVER**. Liver of COD, which, last time we checked, is a fish. Take it from us: they don't write 'Liver' on the side of the bottle just to glam up the product.

Jim in New Zealand: Why is rosé wine generally considered a ladies' drink?

Because it's *pink*. And if men drink anything pink, their testicles immediately turn into a hanging basket of nasturtiums.

Hugo from Hackney: My girlfriend and I spent £17.50 on food while at the cinema this week. Is this a record?

Olly can testify that it is nothing of the sort, having himself spunked £19.75 at the Islington Vue on ice creams, soft drinks and a bag of pick'n'mix. The latter was the real wallet-killer: sweets are priced according to weight, so casually chucking in a couple of strawberry shoelaces – surprisingly dense for their size – can be financially crippling.

However, Olly's appetite for a big bag of chocacolamice* will not be curbed, so he has learned to economise in other ways to keep cinema trips within budget. His current ploy is to book tickets online in advance, 'accidentally' purchasing reduced-price Senior Citizen tickets instead of full-priced Adult ones. Unlike collecting a Student ticket, when one has to present a student ID at the box office, most cinema booking systems work on the assumption that no one – not even those in their late fifties – would ever pretend to be an OAP.

Helen says: Maybe no one would *pretend* to be an OAP, but I know a man who was very happy to be inadvertently mistaken for one: my dad. In his early fifties, he was surprised that his periodic lunches at a favourite fish and chip restaurant were such a bargain. Indeed, they were far cheaper than the listed menu prices . . . because the thoughtful staff had observed his fluffy halo of silver hair and dog-chewed brown tweed hat, guessed him to be some twenty years older than he was, and discreetly charged him for the Pensioners' Discount Special. ▶

---

* Chocacolamice: *noun, pl.* luxurious candy sandwich made from penny sweets, invented by Olly Mann at Letchworth Corner Post Office in 1992. A fizzy cola bottle is the filling, two white chocolate mice the bread.

> Fortunately, Dad is not a vain man (you might have guessed that from the fact he wears hats decorated with dog saliva). More importantly, he is a Jewish man. He was hardly going to complain about the premature concession, so kept schtum about his true age until they offered him the Pensioners' Special puréed and served through a straw. ∎

Michele from the USA: Why are cookies called 'biscuits' in Europe? To us, biscuits are something that come with overly fried food at KFC, not a sweet dessert best dunked in coffee. And if you call cookies 'biscuits', what name do you use for the soft flaky bread we Yanks call biscuits?

We would refer to your American biscuit as a 'scone' (see below), but we doubt a scone has ever graced a KFC in Britain, unless there is a fancypants branch somewhere in the Home Counties which serves a three-course cream tea with Zinger macaroons and deep-fried cucumber sandwiches.

The word 'biscuit' comes from the Latin for 'twice cooked', because in the bad old days before preservatives and biscuit-tins, biscuits used to be cooked then cooked again to ensure they wouldn't go off on long sea voyages or while stuffed into a soldier's shin-guards during a month-long march. Although most modern biscuits are only cooked once (the campaign starts here to rename them 'monocuits'!), snacks such as biscotti still adhere to the old double-baking method, which is why you have to soak them in your half-cap-frapplefrapp for three hours if you don't want to shatter your lower jaw in Starbucks.

Cookies, named after the Dutch word 'koekje' which meant 'little cake', have also been around for centuries – almost as long as the tin of digestives Granny tries to feed us when we pop round for tea. The cookies and the biscuits peacefully coexisted for years, the former a bit fluffier than the latter, until they both migrated to the USA on the *Mayflower*. After the American War of Independence, you defiant little minxes told the British biscuits to shove it, because you'd be calling them cookies from now on. That's Freedom for you.

Ned from Bath: How do you pronounce 'scone'?

In the 'scone' vs. 'scone' debate, we always come down on the side of 'scone'.

Nick from Peckham: On sandwich-packets they never, ever mention that there's a slice of raw, evil, Satan's vomit tomato in the middle. Why the hell is that?

It probably wouldn't be a big seller, would it?

Alex from Northampton: When's my pizza going to arrive?

Approximately thirty seconds after you call the pizza delivery company to give them an earful for being late.

Brendan from London: I ate a hotdog from one of the street vendors at Oxford Circus. It tasted pretty good but smelt of gym socks. Answer me this: how long do I have to live?

The human digestive system is remarkably resilient, so you'll probably survive, even though the average hotdog has equivalent nutritional value to a condom filled with fox faeces. Its main ingredient is something called 'meat slurry', which sounds unappetising enough merely by dint of containing the word 'slurry',

73

but seems even less yummo when you discover that it is a processed meaty swamp begotten by blasting the remaining scraps of tissue off chicken, pig and cow skeletons.

When you consider the reality of chowing down on an artificial cellulose tube stuffed with flesh-sludge, it's no surprise that hotdogs are sold with as many strong-tasting Technicolor condiments as possible. Had Brendan actually died from eating that hotdog, mustard, ketchup and fried onions could all be tried as accessories to murder.

HELEN'S TOP THREE STOMACH-CHURNERS

A non-mover at Number 3: tea at Granny's.
Her generous spreads always included a few unwelcome quirks, but her trademark delicacy was bridge rolls containing cream cheese whipped up with chutney. On paper, this mixture looks like it shouldn't be too bad, but in fact it tastes exactly like acid reflux.

New in at Number 2: American breakfast roulette.
Your magnificent cuisine gives me great pleasure on my holidays to you, America, but sometimes I feel like you're really testing my faith with your crazy food combinations. Exhibit A: a hotel breakfast in Northern California comprised of a red pepper omelette, a ginger cake, whipped cream, orange segments and green olives. No, America. *No.* THESE DO NOT BELONG TOGETHER ON THE SAME PLATE.

Number 1 for seven consecutive years: bad Bergamo birdies.

In the charming medieval town of Bergamo in Northern Italy I met the meal that almost persuaded my stomach to shut up business permanently. It was the last night of our holiday, so my boyfriend and I treated ourselves to a slap-up supper in a local restaurant that on previous visits had shown no signs at all of being a gothic horror show. I ordered quail, which the waiter informed me was off, but that a suitable replacement would be produced.

That suitable replacement turned out to be sparrow. Six sparrows, in fact, served whole and blackened, perched in a line upon a bed of polenta and all staring at me with their burnt-out eyes. Six tiny angels of death. My hitherto unrepentant carnivorism quavered. Half a dozen lives sacrificed for *one* plate of food? I'm aware that one prawn sandwich is the crustacean equivalent of the Battle of the Somme, but it's harder to feel compunction about the mass slaughter of what is tantamount to a pink aquatic insect than it is about the multiple deaths of birds which, as it turned out, don't even taste pleasant. Yes, I did eat it, because the dish had been quite expensive, although I eschewed the proper Italian method of picking them up by the beak and crunching on them whole – I didn't fancy picking fragments of sparrow skull out of my teeth for the rest of the evening. Sorry to be a wimp.

? *Peter from Chicago: Is it possible to have pizzas delivered in the UK?*

Yes, Peter! Even in our olde backwater, 4,000 miles from your pizza-strewn city, we can dial a freephone number and summon a pimply adolescent bearing lukewarm carbohydrates to our doorstep. However, customer-service levels are yet to equal those to which you Yanks are accustomed – we Brits don't kick up a fuss so long as our order arrives within five working days.

Jack from Leeds: Why do toasters need a setting that burns anything to a horrible crisp?

Technically, they need no such thing. All that is actually required of a toaster is that it includes an element powerful enough to toast bread – or, if you are a student, to warm your hands, light your roll-ups and give you something to look at when your Che Guevara poster falls off the wall. Yet, at point of sale, these straightforward items differ wildly in price, from £5 (a beige plastic fire hazard) to £175 (a super-sexy SMEG-Cadillac lovechild). How do these top-line toasters justify their price-tag? The same way the most expensive lawyers do – with a lot of bullshit.

Some are marketed on their 'motorised lift system for effortless removal' (think of all the effort you've wasted in the past, foolishly burdening your delicate fingers with bread!); some have 'a bagel option, to toast one side of a sliced bagel' (a completely different function to a grill, of course); and some boast of up to six 'browning settings'. This gives the impression of choice, the toaster being the obedient servant to its owner's exact toasty desires. In toast, as in life, one man's 'golden brown' is another man's 'charcoal'. Learn to love your fellow humans, Jack, no matter how intolerable you find their beliefs.

Cory from Daytona Beach, Florida: What is the difference between Shepherd's Pie and Cottage Pie and how come the two of them are often confused?

Much like the shepherding and cottaging that inspired them, these two potato-topped mince meals should never be confused. Shepherd's Pie has lamb in it; Cottage Pie has beef in it. That is the difference. Granted, this distinction was only made as recently as the 1870s, and perhaps some folks still haven't heard the news. For decades before that, any old animal-bits stuck under a mound of mash was called 'cottage pie', because potatoes were a cheap crop which poor people could afford – and poor people lived in cottages. How times change: everybody eats potatoes nowadays, and poor people only visit cottages to clean up after rich people. We wonder if, in a hundred years, 'Tower Block Pie' (45 Iceland cocktail sausages, a packet of pickled onion Monster Munch and a bottle of Diamond White) will become a culinary classic too.

FOODS WHICH SHOULD NOT BE CONFUSED. EVER.	
sweet bread (bread that is sweet)	**sweetbreads** (lamb pancreas)
oyster (bivalve mollusc. Famous aphrodisiac)	**oyster** (tooth-rotting ice-cream-van staple. Aphrodisiac only if you are aroused by wafers and sugar comas)
mincemeat (spicy fruity concoction used to fill mince pies)	**minced meat** (minced meat)
crabapple (small sour tree-fruit)	**crab** (crustacean) **apple** (fruit)
bull's eyes (black-and-white-striped minty boiled sweets)	**bull's eyes** (eyes of bulls)

Pratik: Why do people think it's OK to give you those enormous 5kg tins of Celebrations, Roses, Quality Street etc as Christmas gifts? The chocolates taste like crap and there's 5kg of the bollocks! Why?! I don't live in a home with fifteen other people . . .

The reason for these whopping tins is that with the particular confectionaries in question, it is *definitely* quantity that counts, not quality. (Yes, Quality Street is a misnomer, but Quantity Street would be none too encouraging.)

Sure, for the money, you may have preferred one small slab of 85 per cent cocoa solids Ecuadorian single-estate chocolate, but at Christmas such epicurean delicacies are inappropriate. From breakfast to bedtime you are obligated to tear Roses out of their shiny foil frocks and force them down – even though they taste of scented candles – because *if you do not feel full to the point of nausea every waking minute*, the Baby Jesus will cry. And on His birthday, too.

Beckles: Last Saturday whilst I was in the bath, I treated myself to a little snack of corn on the cob. Weird I know, but I'm fine with it. However, it did make me think of a question to ask you. Answer me this: what is the most unusual thing you have ever eaten in the bath?

A cup of tea is as far as we're prepared to go in the realm of bathroom-based consumption, because we don't like to masticate in the same room that we defecate. It just seems unhygienic and

The sheer volume of the sweeties lends an impression of generosity – a false one, since the person bought them in a 2-for-£10 offer at the supermarket, then gave one to you because frankly, Pratik, they don't know you enough (or care) to choose a gift you might actually want or need, but giving you the sweets' value in cash would seem stingy.

wrong, an unsavoury reminder of where that bathsnack will be ending up soon enough.

Beckles is clearly not only less squeamish than us, but also a lot more dextrous. We struggle to read a magazine in the bath without dunking half the page; it is far beyond our capabilities to balance a plateful of a foodstuff which requires two hands to eat. Our minds boggle reading novels in which decadent characters in exotic locales succeed in eating mangoes in the bath, claiming that's the best place to do it in order to avoid juice squirting on your clothes. Such a precaution is never necessary here in England, where mangoes go from rock-hard to rotten without ever stopping at ripe on the way.

Nick: Where does the word, or maybe even the substance, muesli come from? I can't imagine a culture where all that oat and rusk crap is so readily available, and which would come up with a word like 'muesli'.

Evidently Nick can't imagine Switzerland – it's just too neutral for his brain to take in. Muesli was conceived there a century ago by Dr Maximilian Bircher-Benner, who invented it to feed his patients. You might think that poorly cripples, seated on the side of a mountain with fresh Alpine air whistling through their damaged lungs, might prefer a nice hot soup or Kinder Surprise or something, but apparently they couldn't handle real food. So Bircher-Benner whizzed them up some nutritious pap that looked like crushed horse biscuits, and christened it the German word for 'mush'. He could never have predicted that his burdensome mixture would dominate the world of health foods for a hundred years thence. We anticipate the 'wellbeing' revival of other medical methods of the time, such as leeching and routine lobotomies.

Muesli has the reputation of being a bit dull. But sprinkle it with a spoonful of your imagination, and you'll find it's really anything but! Check out our

Five fun things to do with muesli:

1 Smear it all over your face and pretend to be Michael Gambon in *The Singing Detective*.
2 Throw a fresh bowlful onto the pavement, then sit back and watch passers-by dance around it fearing they'll get some sick on their shoes.
3 Muesli sets rock-hard within minutes. Mix up a large batch, and use it to shore up the foundations of your house. Or build a skate ramp with it!
4 Surreptitiously replace the contents of your kids' box of Coco Pops with muesli. The look on their little faces will keep you chuckling all morning!
5 . . . Erm . . .

Sorry. Turns out muesli isn't really fun enough to stretch to five fun things. We tried our best, but there's not much you can do with a bowlful of oats and dried fruit.

Mark from Essex: *Why are digestive biscuits too big to dunk in your tea? The manufacturers of biscuits should make their biscuits mug-sized.*

Get a bigger mug if it upsets you that much.

Joss: *Why is garlic white, but garlic on garlic bread green?*

It isn't – the green bit is chopped parsley. You can't really taste the parsley through a mouthful of garlic, of course, but you put it in anyway, to prevent you confusing your Garlic Bread with your Boring Bread and unwittingly assembling the rankest bread and butter pudding the world has ever tasted.

Nick: In today's state of being constantly aware of potentially offending any race, religion or social group, is the fact that I'm eating a ham bagel going a step too far in anti-Semitism?

No. You *would* be going too far if you threw it at a passing Jew.

Steve in Cheltenham: Should domestic cats be allowed raw meat? When I give our cat raw chicken, it shits liquid for days. I thought, being linked to lions and tigers, that the domestic cat's digestive system could handle the occasional scrag-end of raw chicken-breast. Apparently not – it's decomposed into a vicious brown liquid, capable of stripping paint and removing house guests.

Stop feeding it raw chicken then, you sadist! The issue here is not whether your furry friend's digestive system is able to cope with uncooked meat: cats wouldn't have survived in the wild for generations if they ate only casserole. If, as is quite natural, your cat were to chase after a live chicken, mercilessly rip out its spinal column and take a big juicy bite of pulsing sinew whilst the poor creature was still flapping and squeaking its final breaths (and then leave it there to slowly die, because cats are evil), no vicious brown liquids would emerge from your pet's back passage.

The difference is that the chicken you buy in the supermarket isn't designed to be eaten raw by any beast, because it has not been freshly killed; that poultry titbit you presented to puss as a treat could have been dead for weeks. The British poultry-farm-to-supermarket process is not set up for the diets of lions. Or, indeed, any living thing, aside from salmonella.

Olly says:

I live in a second-floor flat, so my cat Coco lives indoors and uses a litter tray, although one day I intend to train her to crap out of the window onto passers-by. The litter-cleaning process requires me to get down on my hands and knees for a close encounter with her stools, irrefutable proof of my love and affection for this fluffy little ingrate.

One day I was just about to 'do the honours' – an entirely inappropriate euphemism – when I observed that her latest production appeared to be distinctly reddish. I alerted my girlfriend, who insisted upon a more thorough investigation. I duly found myself donning rubber gloves to pull apart a freshly-laid cat turd.

The unidentified red constituent resembled some sort of stretchy tube, which alarmed us both further. Had Coco shat her little guts clean out? Should we call the vet? It was only on closer examination that this mystery ingredient revealed itself to be the strap of my girlfriend's new bikini top. Coco spewed out the rest of it the next day. She is now banned from sleeping in the underwear drawer.

Harvey from Perth: *Where do Heinz 57 Varieties come from? I can only think of three.*

You're right to be dubious – Heinz are 24-carat, pants-on-fire liars! Let's take our tinned soups out onto the streets and stamp them into the gutter (then mop up the mess with some bread rolls and brown sauce. Omnomnom).

Heinz in fact make considerably more than 57 products – they've actually come up with around 6000. Even in the late nineteenth century, when the '57 Varieties' ruse was initiated, Heinz had more than sixty products in their range; 57 was chosen simply because 5 and 7 were 'lucky numbers' for Henry John Heinz and his wife. Years later, these digits are still emblazoned on their iconic, impractical ketchup bottles, and are so entrenched in Heinz's corporate culture that the company's mailing address is PO Box 57, they make a marinade called 'Heinz 57', and their factory shuts down at 57 minutes past each hour so employees can dance around a giant 57m-wide pool of sauce, chanting 'Beanz Meanz Heinz' 57 times before collecting their £57 weekly wage-packet.

'This is not just a marketing wheeze . . .'

At least Heinz has always had a minimum of 57 products on sale whilst boasting of their 57 varieties. Many other companies are far, far fibbier:

- Marks and Spencer's Lochmuir salmon has a picture of a Scottish loch on the front, but Lochmuir itself is a nonexistent town invented by the M&S marketing department as a brand name for fish sourced from various Scottish farms. ▶

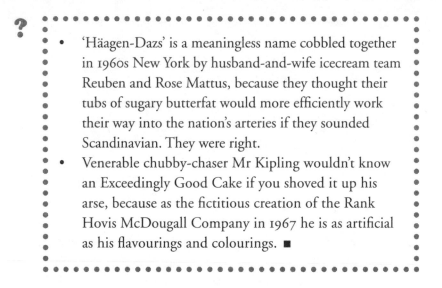

- 'Häagen-Dazs' is a meaningless name cobbled together in 1960s New York by husband-and-wife icecream team Reuben and Rose Mattus, because they thought their tubs of sugary butterfat would more efficiently work their way into the nation's arteries if they sounded Scandinavian. They were right.
- Venerable chubby-chaser Mr Kipling wouldn't know an Exceedingly Good Cake if you shoved it up his arse, because as the fictitious creation of the Rank Hovis McDougall Company in 1967 he is as artificial as his flavourings and colourings. ■

Wayne from St Catharine's, Ontario: 'Spotted dick is a steamed suet pudding containing dried fruit (usually currants) commonly served with custard.' SUET. A.k.a. raw beef or mutton fat, especially the hard fat found around the loins and kidneys.

Are you fucking kidding me? People actually eat this stuff!??!
By choice?
No one's holding a gun to a person's head forcing them to eat it?

Seeing as Wayne is safely tucked up in Ontario, we assume he has never been through the ordeal of traditional British school puds. If he had, he would be relieved that his bowl of dessert contained only beef fat, and not a pound of fag-ash, the brains and feet of a pig, and a couple of naughty children who thought they could skive double Geography without paying the price.

Many adults remain incomprehensibly fond of these doughy logs of nostalgia and insist they continue to be made the 'proper' way. We can think of only one reason why they might persist with suet: animal fats have a higher melting-point than other cook-

ing fats, which, as anyone who has eaten goosefat-roasted potatoes will know, results in a far fluffier texture than any of those
namby-pamby vegetable fats can muster. What mystifies us is that
fluffiness might ever be considered a prized characteristic of a suet
pudding, which is usually stodgier than a cement-mixer full of
the collected works of Sir Walter Scott.

In Days of Yore, suet pudding was far more excusable – Yore's
life-expectancy was far lower anyway, so if the busted arteries
didn't get you, the cholera would. Then, before meat was mass-
produced and the ugly bits thrown away or ground up into
animal-feed, you would have been considered a tittle-brained
fool for wasting any usable part of a butchered beast. Meat was
expensive, so a meal often began with a bowl of broth made of
bones, followed by the suet pudding (a savoury dish in those
days, but many of our sweet-toothed forefathers already enjoyed
spiking it with dried fruit). When the proper meat was wheeled
out for next course, you were already stuffed full of suet so you
didn't scoff all the good stuff in one go when it was supposed to
last the entire season. Peasants would have just made do with the
suet pudding, and knew they should prize the kidney fat for its
superior cooking qualities, rather than boaking at the very idea
as Wayne does.

However, we're actually quite surprised that Wayne even managed to ask us a question about the horror that is suet. Plaudits to
any foreigner who does not die with laughter at the mention of a
pudding effectively named 'pox-riddled penis'.

*Dan: Why does my mum refuse to give me enough sugar in my cof-
fee? I ask for three teaspoons, she refuses by saying, 'Two is more than
enough.' This is the reason why I never accept a hot beverage off my
mother.*

? A little gesture paints a thousand pictures, Dan. Well, perhaps not as many as a thousand, but more than none; here are some of the ones which we're looking at:

1 She is safeguarding your dental health. Hot, sweet drinks have a particularly corrosive effect on the teeth. By refusing you the third spoonful of sugar, she is cutting the negative effects by 33 per cent.

2 Mother knows best! I.e. mother is a control freak. You are her precious baby, she ruptured her perineum bringing you forth into this world, and now you must surrender every aspect of your life to her in return.

3 She finds two sugars more than enough, your grandfather found two sugars more than enough, and his father before him – so why can't you? Because you're adopted! She felt this was the most sensitive way to break it to you.

4 She is of a generation that remembers the days when sugar was rationed. Back then, you'd make one sugar lump last the whole week by clamping it gently between your teeth and sucking your tea through it. You young people, you think sugar grows on trees.

5 She has OCD, which manifests itself in an inability to dole out sugar in odd-numbered spoonfuls.

6 She is using a cunning tactic to ensure she no longer has to run around making you hot drinks.

Paul in Southend: While cooking some brown wholegrain rice to accompany my delicious homemade chilli, I noticed that the cooking instructions on the rice contained the following line: 'Add a pinch of salt, if required, to a large pan of water, and boil'. What are the conditions that make salt a requirement, or, indeed, not? In case you're wondering, I always add salt and have never questioned it . . . until now.

Solids and Liquids

We were always instructed to add salt to a pan of water because it speeds up the boiling time, despite the fact that the amount of salt needed to make a noticeable improvement to the cooking speed of Uncle Ben's would be enough to embalm a hippo. However, there is a useful reason for salinating your rice: as it cooks, rice absorbs the boiling-liquid, along with whatever other flavours are in there. Take a good look at your fridge magnet that bears the homily, 'Never put off till tomorrow what you can do today' and finally understand what it's been trying to tell you all this time: if you leave your seasoning until the rice is cooked, you have to add a lot more salt to achieve the same flavour.

That's the truth, Paul from Southend, but seeing as hitherto you've been trusting enough to do it without even knowing why, we might as well also tell you that if you add a pinch of salt, it makes your balls look bigger. FACT.

Olly says: Saltwater still has the capacity makes me wince, and not just because of my ill-fated excursion to the Dead Sea (any prick who tells you hypersaline water works wonders for psoriasis has clearly not dipped their reddened scalp into it – a wasps' nest would have hurt less). The briny trauma that haunts me still occurred in my undergraduate days, when I shared a house with two student medics. When not attending lectures, writing for the student paper or bashing my head against the wall because no one would sleep with me, I liked to indulge in typical academic pursuits, such as watching *Open House with Gloria Hunniford* in my pyjamas. ▶

One day, engrossed in an especially gripping sequence – an interview with Michael Ball, a baking demonstration and a performance by Daniel O'Donnell – I realised I required rehydration, but couldn't bear to tear myself away from the box. Fortunately somebody had left a glass of water on the table next to me. My housemates surely wouldn't object if I drank it. The glass was warm, but for some reason this didn't strike me as weird.

Shock: the water was intensely salty; salty and tepid. Like a mouthful of the Adriatic. Revolting. I swallowed quickly, and tried my best to forget all about it.

Later that afternoon, about halfway through *Miss Marple*, my housemate was rooting about in the lounge. 'Has anyone seen my pus water?' she asked.

Until that moment, I hadn't known that words alone could be powerful enough to make me retch, yet on hearing her question, a salty residue leapt from the pit of my stomach to the back of my throat.

'Er, what?' I enquired, as innocently as I could.

'I've got a wound on my finger,' she said, cheerfully. 'I've been dipping it in saline to draw out the pus.'

The moral here is that English literature students and trainee doctors should live in *separate houses*. ∎

Sam of Leeds: Is it possible to eat a pasty on the move while retaining any kind of dignity?

No way. It is hard enough when one is stationary, but not even Grace Kelly could have maintained her customary stateliness with flakes of pastry all down her front; and had a blob of gravy dripped onto her Givenchy lapel as she rushed across a station concourse gobbling down her snack, we doubt Hitchcock would have looked at her twice.

Polish Greg: One of the traditional Polish dishes is a soup called Flaki, which is made from cleaned strips of beef or chicken tripe. I know that it sounds disgusting, but I love it and I would kill for a bowl of hot, spicy soup. Is there a dish which sounds disgusting, but you really love?

Most foreign delicacies sound revolting if you just list their raw ingredients: 'sushi' sounds alluringly exotic, whereas 'raw eel, enveloped in cold, vinegary rice, rolled in seaweed sheets and dipped in hurty snot-coloured horseradish' seems rather less appetising. So we're sure that the tripe slop which Greg loves is indeed delicious, and that all our favourite dishes would sound disgusting to someone, somewhere.

Helen regularly partakes of Bovril on toast, something Olly could not contemplate putting near his mouth, not even if he were kidnapped and forced to take part in *The 1940s House* and there was nothing else to eat except powdered eggs and Brylcreem. Olly's own questionable gastronomic preferences include adding mayonnaise to *everything* (lasagne, soup, trifle), and chewing his fingernails (if you can call that a 'dish'), although he recently stopped doing this when he realised that the persistent pain in his gums was caused by a six-week-old fingernail lodged between his teeth.

But Olly's dad holds the title of King of Eating Things Which Sound Digusting: *vide* his love of 'Imitation Calf's-Foot Jelly', four words which don't sit easily together on the label, never mind in a human stomach. His former trade as a butcher left him entirely unsqueamish around animal-bits, a trait further evidenced by his preference for dipping chicken's feet into his chicken soup then sucking the gritty bits out, the toes dangling from his mouth as he asks for the salt.

George from Aberdeenshire: Why is it impossible for me to eat a Love Heart sweet without reading what's on it first?

Because you are possessed of curiosity, an integral neurobiological feature that equips us humans to develop as a race. Reading Love Heart slogans is as natural and instinctual as running your hands over scarves that you have no intention of buying, or scoffing at a stranger's taste in decor when peering through their front window as you stroll past. If we ever saw someone pop a Love Heart straight into their gob without at least *glancing* down at the message first, we would shoot to kill.

Donna: Which is posher, brown sauce or red sauce?

Brown sauce is clearly posher: it's got tamarind in it! Also, posh people would rather give up complaining about the foxhunting ban than call tomato ketchup 'red sauce'. When *they* say 'red sauce', they are referring to raspberry coulis.

Morgan: Why are eggs considered dairy products when they have nothing to do with milk, cows or anything dairy?

Milky products and eggs both used to be kept in the cool storage rooms known as dairies, even though they issue forth from different beasts. The platypus is the only creature capable of producing both eggs and milk, which is why it's so useful to keep one as a pet for when eggnog season rolls around.

Brendan from Cork: Is Turkish Delight actually from Turkey? My friend says it is but I don't believe him, because he's an idiot.

Yes, it is. Now who's the idiot?

Ian from Bedfordshire: Why is it that oilseed rape has such a horrible name?

Linguistics can be cruel, Ian, and this is a punishment we wouldn't wish on even our least favourite crop. An innocent member of the mustard family, poor old oilseed rape takes its unfortunate name from the Latin word 'rapum', meaning 'turnip'. Meanwhile the sex crime is from the unrelated Latin verb 'rapere', which meant 'to seize or take by force'. Like many other words that sounded similar to one another, the two rapes entered the English language in the Middle Ages and over time became the same word. As far as we know, it wasn't because there were medieval trends for sexually violating mustard, or for planting women in yellow fields for use in biodiesel and animal feed.

Surely anyone in their right mind should have realised that, once the crime of rape caught on, it was time to rename the crop, which other countries sensibly refer to as 'canola'. Yet another symptom of Broken Britain!

Liz: Who invented marshmallows and why?

The ancient Egyptians came up with them; as to why, we can only speculate, but it was probably because they liked eating sweeties. Their prototype marshmallows were a confection of honey thickened with the sap of the marsh mallow plant, whose roots run plentifully with a thick syrupy gunge known as mucilage. This charming-sounding substance is not only useful for making gummy candy, but also possesses healing properties: it could soothe a troubled bowel or suppurating boil, and in the nineteenth century, doctors took to whipping it up with egg whites and sugar and spooning the firmed-up mixture down the sore throats of invalids.

The invalids must have kept on scoffing marshmallows after their invalidity was over, because it wasn't long before commercial manufacturers started making them, replacing the mucilage with gum arabic and gelatine to give them longer shelf-life and make them easier to mass-produce in factories. Thus the marshmallow's surprise status as a health food was, alas, revoked, only to be replaced by other nutritious snacks like pretzels, diet sodas and chocolate-coated cereal bars.

Chris from March, Cambridgeshire: What's the difference between a cheese sandwich and a cheese toastie? My missus has a go at me when I want a cheese toastie instead of a cheese sandwich; what the fuck is up with that?

What difference indeed, Chris? For are they not both cheese and bread, after all, just as we humans are all flesh and blood beneath it all, no matter what our colour or creed? Just as a soufflé and a hardboiled egg must be EXACTLY THE SAME THING? For goodness' sake, man! The fact that you have even asked this question demonstrates that you are a bit backward, so we are going to have to spell it out for you:

A cheese sandwich is cold cheese between slices of cold bread.

A toastie is hot, molten cheese between slices of hot crisp bread. DO YOU SEE?

Furthermore, since you said 'toastie' rather than 'toasted cheese sandwich', we're going to add that it should have been made in a toastie-maker, pressing the layers together into a sharp-cornered envelope of cheese lava.

The reason your missus objects to being asked for one is because cleaning dried melted cheese out of the hinges of a sandwich toaster is a right pain. And because she resents being treated like your cheese toastie slave. And because you are clearly a total idiot.

EXAM TIME: HOW CHEESY ARE YOU?

CHEESE HISTORY

Cheese is one of Britain's all-time favourite conversation topics, after the weather and whether Bruce Forsyth will ever be awarded a knighthood. It has evidently always been thus, so, answer us this: which cheese was mentioned in the Domesday Book?

a. Cheddar cheese
b. Cheshire cheese
c. Kraft Cheese Strings
d. Knob cheese

ANSWER: *B. No mention of Branston Pickle alongside, surprisingly.*

CHEESE LINGUISTICS

When people hijack the good name of cheese to pep up their patter, we get really cheesed off. Answer us this: which of these cheesy slang phrases has NOTHING TO DO with cheese?

a. 'Cheesewagons' = American schoolbuses
b. 'The Big Cheese' = the bossfella
c. 'Cutting the cheese' = to break wind
d. 'Cheeseheads' = natives of Wisconsin or the Netherlands

ANSWER: B. 'Cheesewagons' are yellow, as is cheese. 'Cutting the cheese' refers to the mutual malodourousness of cheese and farts. 'Cheeseheads' are so-called because Wisconsin and the Netherlands are centres of cheese manufacture. Whereas the 'cheese' in 'Big Cheese' is a false etymology, deriving from the Persian or Hindi word 'chiz', meaning 'a thing'.

MATHS

Answer us this: how much milk does it take to make one kilo of Cheddar?

a. 5 litres
b. 10 litres
c. 27 litres
d. Don't be silly! Cheddar isn't made with *milk*!

ANSWER: *B*

GEOGRAPHY

Speaking of Cheddar, numerous American pals of ours believe the Somerset town of Cheddar was named after the cheese rather than the other way round. So answer us this: which of these cheese manufacturing facts is false?

a. Shropshire Blue originated in Scotland
b. Stilton cheese has never been made in Stilton, Cambridgeshire
c. Former athlete Zola Budd and Sonic Youth's Kim Gordon have their own cheesemaking company called Gordonzola
d. Cornish Yarg is wrapped in nettle leaves. It's pretty, and keeps thieving hands at bay!

ANSWER: *C. But don't you think that would be a winner?*

Cheese is widely believed to give you nightmares. But actually tryptophan, an amino acid present in cheese, has been shown to reduce stress and induce sleep. Answer us this: which of these cheese statements is not another bloody great lie?

a. Henry VIII commissioned a full-size statue of Anne Boleyn made of cheese, then ate its head
b. Red Leicester was the official cheese of the Labour Party under Neil Kinnock
c. Courtney Love's tip for staying slim is to never eat cheese – although you'd think all that heroin probably helped to keep her trim
d. Endemol are developing a reality TV series following eight minor celebrities in which they eat nothing but cheese and Chupa Chups for six weeks.

ANSWER: *C. Courtney Love thinks cheese is evil. We think she should concentrate on her more pressing problems.*

IF YOU SCORED

0–2 points: You are as cheesy as Tangy Cheese Doritos. Must try harder.
3–4 points: You are as cheesy as a mild Stilton. Respectable.
5 points: Congratulations – you are as cheesy as David Hasselhoff eating a cheesecake made of extra-mature Vieux Boulogne.

Matthew from Loughborough: My wife bought a bag of Cadbury's Mis-Shapes at the weekend, and we found a bag full of distorted strawberry and orange creams. I thought to myself, who likes these? Why do they make them? Even my late grandmother used to avoid them if given a chance. So answer me this: who likes strawberry and orange creams as their chocolates of choice?

We suspect that sometimes foul flavours are created just to make the rest of the selection seem tastier by comparison (see also: Thornton's white chocolate truffle flavoured with lemon, which doubles as a handy emetic). During her sweetie-deprived childhood, on the twice-yearly dip into the Quality Street, Helen was duped into eating the strawberry creams by their pretty red and green foil. As the lowest seed in the Zaltzman pecking order, it was between that or the crunchy coconut one, a choice on a par with that forced upon the victim in *Se7en* who either has to slice off her own nose, or top herself.

By purchasing Mis-Shapes, Matthew's wife gambled that for some reason the manufacturer would reward her with a big budget bag full of caramel barrels, fudge diamonds, or those nice purple ones in the shape of Napoleon's hat. At THAT price? Pure naivety. At the Chocolate Casino, the House *always* wins.

Martin the Sound Man's Science Corner

Hello readers! I'm Martin, *Answer Me This!*'s resident musician and sound engineer. I also have a PhD in quantum physics, so Helen and Olly wheel me out whenever they receive a science question, because frankly they wouldn't know a quark if one slapped them on the bum. Which they wouldn't even notice, because quarks are really small. Anyway, they've handed over the book to me for a couple of pages so that I can answer some of your scientific queries while they rearrange their dolls'-house furniture or whatever. So strap in for a bumpy ride through the world of Science:

Steve and Lynne*: What happens if you add Dettol to Yakult? Would it just become normal yoghurt?*

No. Don't drink it! It will be, at best, disgusting. I would expect the Dettol to kill the Yakult's so-called 'good bacteria' (don't get me started), but it is also quite likely to kill you too.

Greg in Swindon*: Which is harder, brain surgery or rocket science?*

Brain surgery. Rocket science was invented by Nazis in the Second World War, and all their other ideas were pretty stupid, so if they can do it, it can't be that hard.

Adam, MYP for Horsham and Mid Sussex: *Was the trip I made today to Thorpe Park with my AS physics class in ANY way justified, or just an excuse for students and teachers to ride some rollercoasters?*

Totally justified! Physics is not one of the more popular subjects, so we have to bribe kids to do it. But actually, in my professional scientist opinion, there are excellent physics-observing opportunities at Thorpe Park. The swingboat demonstrates how the oscillation period of a pendulum depends on its mass and length. 'Colossus' teaches you all about centripetal force and the way it balances with gravity when you're looping-the-loop. And the Flying Fish shows you that, um, hallucinogens and engineering aren't the best playmates.

Ian in Wakefield: *If you swallow helium, your voice goes all funny. If you put helium up your arse, would your farts sound funny?*

Of course they would, Ian, because farts ALWAYS sound funny. Scientific fact. Would they sound amusingly squeaky? Sadly not. Sound travels through helium faster than through air, amplifying the higher frequencies in your voice, and producing the famous chipmunk effect. Whereas the noise of your farts is made by the oscillation of your sphincter as your gut gales force their way out, so even if you had a rectum full of helium, your guffs would sound much the same as usual. You could try farting into a jar filled with helium – that might sound funny. It would definitely look funny.

Joe in Streatham: *When they try to defuse a bomb in action movies, why do they say 'Cut the red wire' or 'Cut the blue wire'? Surely it's just a circuit so if you cut all the wires it would stop working?*

You shouldn't assume a circuit will break if you cut all its wires. Doing that might create a short circuit, activating the detonation mechanism: an even faster route to KABOOM. Plus, any bomb designer worth his Semtex is hardly going to design a bomb that is easily defused, so they'll usually include little tricks to trip up defusal experts.

It's a bitter pill to swallow, but action movies rarely resemble the truth. Take it from me, it's quite hard to outrun an explosion in a corridor, escape a hail of machine-gun fire without a blemish, or wear a white vest without looking like a total pillock. And I don't remember Indiana Jones carefully marking out his archaeological digs with a grid of string, then gently scraping at the earth with a trowel for months and months and months. Veracity is the casualty of storytelling; so, movies have a red wire/blue wire scenario as a dramatic tool to create tension for the viewer without the heroes getting bogged down in the real complexities of a bomb's workings. Then they can get on with the important business of driving motorbikes and shooting baddies in slow motion.

Nick from Tadley: *I am allergic to all dairy, nuts, and shellfish, and any consumption of these may result in death. Answer me this, how do allergies kill me?*

Your body goes into anaphylactic shock, your airways swell up and you slowly asphyxiate unless someone comes along with an emergency adrenaline shot. Basically, Nick, your body is trying to tell you you're not cut out for this world. Sorry to be the bearer of bad news.

Dovy: *Do you think there is life on other planets?*

Yes. Given the size of the universe, it seems statistically almost certain that there's a form of life on another planet, and it would be arrogant to assume otherwise. There is already evidence of liquid water elsewhere in our solar system, which on Earth is a prerequisite for life, so we can guess that there's someone or something churning around out there. Whether we will ever meet intelligent life, or anything which has evolved beyond a single cell, is less clear. The other question is whether we would even recognise it if we saw it, intelligence being an ever less valued attribute in today's society. I'm a pariah, Dovy, I really am.

Wendy: Why are there 360 degrees in a circle? Wouldn't it be more logical for there to be 100, and divide it up that way? 360 seems a rather random number to me.

If it's logic you want, Wendy, then you may prefer the units that we physicists more typically use nowadays, which are called 'radians'. There are 2Π radians in a complete circle, so each radian is about 57.2958 degrees. 360 isn't looking so inconvenient to you now, is it?

Graham from Canada: I recently discovered a website that claims to have X-ray goggles that operate by sending out small bits of radiation and other technical shit, should I buy them? They are quite expensive . . .

Don't buy them. They won't work. By which I mean you wouldn't be able to see through ladies' blouses with them.

Sexy Time

Turn down the lights, turn down the bed, turn on your bedside lamp and read our guidance on love, romance and Doing It. Make the ladies love you; make the guys fall at your feet; make sure you clean up afterwards.

Jordan from Edinburgh: My girlfriend and I are going on our first solo train journey in a few weeks and we've mutually decided that we want to have sex on the train. So answer me this, what is best way to have sex in the train toilets without getting caught?

The problem is not so much you getting caught, as you catching something. We're assuming you have never actually seen a train toilet, otherwise there is no way you would contemplate getting busy in one. Imagine a normal public convenience – surely libido-killing enough at the best of times – then factor in that a convenience on a train will have been shat and pissed on by hundreds of people who have motion sickness, caught the runs from the buffet car, or simply can't accurately aim their urethras at a lavatory pan that is travelling along a bumpy track at 100 miles an hour.

We can think of only one means of train sex which doesn't have us drawing up vows of celibacy. Since you're in Edinburgh, book yourselves on to the Edinburgh–London sleeper, and enjoy a night of passion tinged with the romance of the bygone Golden Age of the Railways. Just make sure to secure a private berth, as after all that effort, you would not want your railway romp to be ruined by a snoring businessman in the opposite bunk.

Andy from Essex: Why is being a spinster seen as a bad thing, but being a bachelor is seen as a good thing?

You are quite right to point out this inequity. Nobody thinks, Oh, look at that poor George Clooney, pushing 50 and without a wife to look after him, his only solace jetskiing on Lake Como with a porn star again. Yet when Renee Zellweger hit 40 without a husband to speak of, the world assumed she would henceforth spend all her evenings alone, carding wool and weeping over the demise of her sexual organs.

Let's examine this disparity more closely, with some side-by-side stereotyping opposite . . .

And now for some reality. Unmarried women are no less likely to be happy and fun. Unmarried men are no less likely to yearn for companionship and domesticity. And, you know what, Miss Marple's HOT! (Olly surveys the room for agreement. Olly gestures at the photo of Joan Hickson he carries in his wallet. Olly tucks his stiffy under his waistband and admits he is alone in this.)

History supports our view, or at least some periods of it. In medieval times, spinsters had it much better than married women: they were more likely to be educated, less likely to die in childbirth, and, unlike wives, were allowed to have their own land, affording them a powerful position in society. So, what happened in the intervening centuries to reverse their fortunes?

Frigging Martin Luther happened, that's what. When in 1517 the grumpy Teutonic priest published his *95 Theses*, little could he have expected that he was precipitating the Protestant Reformation, still less that he was condemning single women of the future to a life of Fair Isle cardigans and seed cake. All he had intended

Typical . . .	BACHELOR	SPINSTER
portrayal in culture	James Bond	Miss Marple
image	swinging	wizened
habitat	bars, airports, strip clubs	church halls, beetle drives, yarn shops
transport	sports car	bicycle with a basket, or shoppers' bus
foodstuff	Supernoodles	a dry biscuit
smell	aftershave. The lingering scent of Ladies	lavender. Mustiness. Or that purple perfume from the Body Shop which smells of lavender AND mustiness
pet	pets are too much commitment	seventeen cats
death	on his 101st birthday, at the climactic point of a romp with a pair of 22-year-old Swedish masseuses	from loneliness

was to take down the Roman Catholic Church, delivering smack-down after smackdown to all that the pious held dear, including celibacy – 'One cannot be unmarried without sin,' he cried, before relieving a lifetime of blue balls by marrying an ex-nun and begetting five children sharpish.

Thus marriage became all the rage amongst sixteenth-century god-botherers, and spinsters were henceforth viewed with suspicion and contempt. Shakespeare and co. cast them as ugly, cranky, warty killjoys for the next several centuries, until *Sex and the City* came along and recast them as fatuous self-obsessed neurotics. Meanwhile, unfettered by domestic nonsense or shrewish wives, bachelors went from strength to strength, earning themselves such glamorous adjectives as 'eligible' and, um, 'gay' (back when 'gay' meant happy, rather than the type of bachelor who is romantically interested in other bachelors).

George: How can you tell if an old person used to be hot?

If Lauren Bacall and Kathleen Turner are anything to go by, you can tell if an old person used to be hot because they look like gargoyles and sound like strimmers.

It would be great if there were a more scientific method of finding out, like cutting through a tree and counting its rings to determine its age. But there isn't. The most accurate barometer is when you're belting out carols in an old people's home at Christmas and suddenly get an erection, but don't know why: it's proof that the old codger or codgerette in your eyeline used to be a total fittie.

Cherry: Why the hell do I fancy a guy only after *one of my friends is going out with him? Before they started going out, I never noticed him; now I think he is really hot and can't stop looking at him.*

When some goofy chemist first produced a vat of brightly-coloured slime, no one was interested in it as a commercial possibility. But as soon as canny marketing boffins put this pointless goop into little plastic containers and called it 'Fart Pot', the world's children were clamouring to piss away their pocket money on a tooting tub of tomfoolery.

Similarly, Cherry, we suspect your friend's boyfriend hasn't actually turned overnight from Johnny Rotten to Johnny Depp. Though once you found him less alluring than a wet weekend in Telford, simply by attracting the interest of someone else he has proved himself romantically viable and is thus rebranded in your eyes. His pimples suddenly seem to be beauty spots, his sweaty insoles the sweetest pong in the perfumery, his adolescent moustache the proscenium arch over a barnstorming production of *Chicago*.

You're being lazy. Your friend has procured a man, thus saving you the bother of having to pick out a suitable one yourself from all the other millions of chaps. Plus, she is saddled with the task of training him, so if you steal him he will already be fully operational.

We suggest it's not *him* you want; it's the excitement of contraband. By yearning for a man who is unavailable, you are hurling yourself into the same hackneyed situation as those 'women who go for bastards' we're always reading about: the relationship is doomed, so you can have all the dramatic fun of an epic romance minus the tiresome extras like joint mortgages, arguing over whose turn it is to take out the recycling, or committing your soul for eternity.

Unless, Cherry, you want to be branded a Scarlet Woman and live with the guilt for ever, don't poach this man. Few fellows are worth breaching the tenets of friendship for, and with a little self-discipline, you can make your passion wilt. Every time you want to gaze longingly at him, you should do a Google Image search for 'prolapsed anus' and stare intently at the results. Whenever you find yourself daydreaming of him, eat a tablespoon of mustard powder. Supplement this regime with the traditional ardour-cooling cold showers. If you still can't quench your own adoration, you must instead ensure that there's no way he will make an advance himself: we suggest you give up brushing your teeth.

HELEN'S TOP FIVE MEN BENEFITING FROM THE REFLECTED ATTRACTIVENESS OF LADIES

5. DAVID MELLOR: Someone *willingly* had sex with the wibbly-faced Tory? Blimey. What's his secret?

4. LEMBIT OPIK: I thought the alien-obsessed erstwhile Lib Dem was batting above his weight when he was engaged to weathergirl Siân Lloyd. And then he dumped her for a Cheeky Girl half his age, whom he then replaced with a 22-year-old bra model. Lord knows what they chatted about over the breakfast table.

3. ANNE HECHE: I'm aware she is not a man; but were it not for her three-year relationship with Ellen DeGeneres, I and the rest of the world would not have been aware of her at all.

2. MARK CROFT: Despite looking like an evil pebble and being apparently devoid of any merit in character, the former Mr Kerry Katona actually had ladies fighting over him! For years Kerry repeatedly took him back, despite his alleged affairs with lap-dancers AND HER OWN MUM. Plaintive women kept popping up in the *News of the World* claiming he was their absent babydaddy. And yet, the world over, very decent men struggle to lose their virginities. What's *wrong* with women?

1. JUSTIN TIMBERLAKE: I know he's done very well for himself, and is nicer to look at than a rotting turnip. BUT. Had Britney not selected him as her first official boyfriend, would he have been declared *People* Magazine's 14th Sexiest Man Alive in 2007? No. He would just be the curly-haired one from that group that wasn't the Backstreet Boys.

Beth: Fuck-buddy relationships are OK, right?

Yes, if the parameters are very clearly established. Remember how annoyed you felt when you agreed to split lunch with a friend and only ordered the Earlybird special, but your buddy went for two starters, side dish, extra bread rolls, pudding and petits fours? You must avoid the sexual equivalent. If you're both unambiguous in understanding that it's just about casual sex, there's no reason it shouldn't work, so long as:

1 Your chosen bedmate is not a psychopath who will later stab you through the chest (cf. Tom Jones's 'Delilah');
2 You have nothing in common apart from physical needs, so won't ever want to take it further (cf. *Pretty Woman*);
3 You don't shag someone who then marries the brother of your best mate who is dying of AIDS, thus compelling you to confess everything to your wife and family (cf. *One Night Stand*).

James from Moline, Illinois: Does the Queen spit or swallow?

We see you are an American, James, and perhaps still recovering from the national trauma of Bill Clinton's Oral Office; but show some respect! Our beloved monarch is pure and chaste, her four children having been gestated in an ermine uterus in a special lab beneath Windsor Castle. The only royal jelly she gulps down is from bees, not Prince Philip. Plus she has servants to perform unsavoury tasks on her behalf, so there is probably a fellatio butler somewhere on the staff.

Nonetheless, it's worth remembering that the Queen has spent a lifetime being discreet. At her age, she'd surely prefer a quiet night in with a copy of the *Racing Post* to watching the cast of

Holby City murdering 'You Can Leave Your Hat On' at the Royal Variety Performance; but she always does her public duty, whatever her mood. If, therefore, a scenario unfolded in which the Queen had no choice but to chow down, we predict she would simply close her eyes, imagine she was at another of those unpleasant banquets at the Kyrgyzstan embassy and imbibe politely. She would allow no trickles to sully her royal visage, as defacing the Queen is a punishable offence.

But you forget the third option. Judging by her fondness of Crown Jewels, we suspect the Queen might actually be quite partial to a pearl necklace. We refer you to that neglected third verse of the British national anthem, which declares: 'Thy choicest gifts in store,/On her be pleased to pour'. Have you never wondered why our stamps and banknotes only show her from the neck up?

Marie: What is the origin of the phrase 'carnal knowledge'? I know 'carn' refers to meat, as in 'chilli con carne', 'carnivorous' etc – this surely can't be a reference to man-meat?

Call the *New Scientist*! Marie has stumbled upon the germ of a groundbreaking new theory as to why the dinosaurs are extinct: because the carnivores were too busy fellating each other to reproduce. If only palaeontologists were more smutty, they wouldn't have wasted all those years blaming meteor strikes, ice ages and prehistoric viruses.

Marie's dirty mind is instead leading her astray linguistically, because in culinary terms 'carne' merely refers to normal, non-wang meat, unless Armin Meiwes is doing the cooking. Historically, 'carn-' does also refer to flesh, as anyone who has seen *Candyman 2: Farewell to the Flesh* will remember, thanks to a scary voice growling 'Farewell to the flesh!' whenever the New Orleans Mardi

Gras carnival is mentioned, thereby injecting a soothing note of philology into an otherwise unprepossessing horror sequel.

We have our old schoolfriend Latin to thank for the 'carn-' bit of 'carnal', and the coyness of England of the Middle Ages for the 'knowledge'. The Bible was considered a very rude book back then, just as in the 1920s *Lady Chatterley's Lover* was considered to be something other than 300 pages of YAWN. Times change, y'all. When the Bible was finally translated into English – quite a feat, as anyone trying to do it was liable to be burnt to death – it was peppered with a hilarious selection of euphemisms. Genitals were replaced by 'loins', 'fountains', 'secrets', 'hinge', 'feet' and 'uncomely parts', while sex was bashfully indicated by such verbs as 'went', 'humbled' and 'knew'.

As to why 'carnal' and 'knowledge' were finally joined together like fountains to hinges: we imagine it was because otherwise the term is so oblique that anyone reading the phrase 'Adam knew Eve' in the Book of Genesis is going to be utterly flummoxed as to how they got around to begetting the entire human race.

Natasha from Cambridge: Why do I only read Cosmo for the bits where they talk about sex?

You're hardly going to read it for their insight into the Kashmir conflict, are you?

Paul from Southend: Why is it complimentary to describe a woman as a bombshell, but insulting to describe her as a battleaxe? Why are bombs sexy, yet axes aren't?

Sexiness and war are more customary psychological bedfellows than sexiness and chopping, which is why *Top Gun* is more popular at Netflix than *Pippi Longstocking*.

? Battleaxes have never sounded very sexy, being heavy, double-headed, and wielded by Teutonic warriors. Bombshells don't sound especially arousing either, but they managed to get sexy when Allied troops used to paint voluptuous ladies onto them, to remind themselves of female company and distract themselves from the harsh realities of World War II. Virgin Atlantic later copied the gimmick and emblazoned retro pin-up-type ladies across their aeroplane noses, even though nobody wants to think about a deadly bombing raid when they're crossing the ocean at 500 mph and trying to watch *Everybody Loves Raymond*.

Marc: I'm 18, male and have been given the chance to be in a straight, professionally done porno. Should I take it, or will it hang over my head until one day my mates stumble across it and say 'Hey, he looks familiar . . .?' The money's not too bad.

Contemplate at length whether you are amenable to having sex for money, then contemplate at even greater length whether would feel comfortable explaining this escapade to, say, your future wife and/or grandchildren. If so, well, you're 18 and, what with the current job market, it's a fairly solid career move – even in the bleakest economic times, people will always need material to beat off to. And just imagine the raised eyebrows at your school reunion when everyone finds out that you're the only person in the class who didn't become a solicitor or actuary!

Do bear in mind that those mates of yours will, sooner or later, come across your porno adventures, so reconcile yourself to the idea of them seeing you in a state of tumescence, covered in fake tan and reciting the cheesiest dialogue since *Eldorado* was decommissioned; and be prepared for them to feel a bit scared, horrified, or worst of all, aroused.

Rebecca from London: Why is it your friends always think they have the right to match you up with someone?

Ungrateful Rebecca! Your noble friends are trawling their stock of dearest acquaintances to find you the perfect mate, filtering rigorously to ensure that they only present the premium specimens of humankind for your consideration, because all they want is for you to meet your ideal match and dwell in bliss for evermore. Yet you interpret this as meddlesome, patronisingly implying that you are neither happy being single nor capable of finding your own dates! Well . . . OK, you may have a point.

Thing is, we humanoids often suffer from a nigh irresistible urge to pair our fellows up. Pairs of anything are nice and tidy; just ask Noah. Matchmaking plans are not always a completely terrible idea: for instance, if we were to set up Friend A with Friend B, before they have even met, they have at least one thing in common – the fact that they know us. Marriages have been founded on less.

If your aspiring matchmakers are single, they might be acting out of a selfless urge to attain for you the becoupled happiness their own lives lack, perhaps nursing a hope that if they succeed, karma will supply them with their own dreamboats in return. Or maybe they have merely spotted someone they think you would really get along with. Nothing sinister in that.

If, however, you are in the clutches of a Cupid-playing couple, they may be using you to live vicariously. They miss the single life, the thrill of a fledgling romance; but rather than risking their joint mortgage by having affairs, they're using YOU as their pawn, so that when they've shacked you up with someone, they can bask in both your reflected new-relationship glow and the pleasure of a Job Well Done. This couple might be so happy in their own relationship that they can't bear the thought of anyone

? languishing alone; alternatively they are the opposite of happy, and can't bear the thought of anyone else having more fun than them.

Or perhaps your friends have put up with months and months of you moaning that you're single and lonely and so they're trying something, *any*thing, to make you shut up. We all got tired of Bridget Jones ten years ago, Rebecca.

Charlie from London: My wife and I have been invited by a couple we know from work to join the swinging lifestyle. I am very interested and my wife hasn't said 'No' outright, which intrigues me. I am quite keen to get a legitimate 'Yes', as I have been seeing the other woman for a few months now. I will stop seeing her if my wife says 'No', but would rather not. How do I convince my wife?

Cripes. We would be fascinated to know how you broached this subject with your wife – most men are too terrified even to ask their spouses for a blowjob on their birthday. If it was as honest and direct a conversation as you suggest, and she didn't answer strongly in the affirmative, she's probably not overly keen, and the last thing you would want for a successful swing is any sense that you forced her into it. So try to indoctrinate your wife sub-liminally, Derren Brown-style. Here's our plan of action:

- Set your ringtone to 'Swinging on a Star' by Bing Crosby.
- Start leaving your car keys in a fruit bowl in the living room.
- End all your anecdotes with 'Swings and roundabouts, eh? That's life'.
- Offer to take her to swing dance classes.
- Plant a giant clump of pampas grass in your front garden.
- Watch *The Ice Storm* together until she learns to enjoy it.
- Start shouting several other people's names during sex.

But even if your wife does come round to the idea, why embark upon this adventure with a couple from *work*? Such a transgressive blurring of the boundary between business and pleasure is simply not sensible. Imagine those 'watercooler moments': 'Did you see *Dancing on Ice* last night? Where were you thinking of having lunch today? Do you fancy four-way fellatio this weekend?' Few words make for less welcome pillow-talk than 'Can you have that report on my desk first thing tomorrow?' We're not convinced this arrangement will end well. But, by golly, it's a novel approach to team-building exercises.

Victor from Portsmouth: Why do lesbians use strap-ons? Why don't they just have sex with a man in the first place?

Because they enjoy the sensation of something hard penetrating their lady-parts, but are not physically attracted to men. That goes for many heterosexual women, too.

Anon: Why is it that whenever I travel on the bus I inexplicably get an erection?

It's probably just the vibrations of the vehicle. Because we've racked our brains and cannot think of a single thing that is sexually stimulating about public transport. Not one. And if you can think of one, you should be neutered, for everybody's safety.

Tom from Luxembourg: When I was four, I liked a girl in my class – her name was Vanessa. Now I fancy a girl in my new class and her name is also Vanessa. The problem is my mum is called Vanessa. Is it normal that I only fancy girls that have the same name as my mum?

Past Times

Not the gift shop, silly – history! If Granny and Grandad are too drunk, doddery or dead to tell you all about the olden days, turn to us instead. We're totally qualified, having seen both *Gladiator* and *Robin Hood: Prince of Thieves* and owning several cardigans between us.

Elliot from Redcar: What is the use of a hooked hand for a pirate, really? Wouldn't it just get in the way? Wouldn't a series of attachments be easier? I suggest a telescope, a sword, a fishing rod, a selection of cutlery and crocodile repellent spray.

Fun as a range of changeable screw-in attachments would be, Elliot, storage space is at a premium on a ship, which is why pirates are in fact masters of the supremely practical two-in-one device. For instance, they invented 'walking the plank', a punishment so efficient that seconds after a traitor is forced to his watery grave, the instrument of death can be repurposed as a sturdy docking platform without so much as a wipedown, and the crew can toddle off to shore for a post-kill coffee and cupcake.

Similarly, hooked hands actually have multiple useful applications. They can be used for carrying shopping-baskets, zip-lining along the rigging, gutting fish, gouging out eyes, ripping open throats, slashing nostrils, rupturing testicles . . . And let's not forget their primary purpose: *they look scary*. This is of paramount concern to the limbless professional pirate. Back when decent plastic and rubber prosthetics were still a pipe dream, and disability discrimination laws were yet to grace the statute books, it was hard to look like a fearless bully of the high seas when you had a hand-shaped block of wood stuck up your sleeve. But, when the appendage on the end of their arm was a big, sharp, hooky *hook*, then, ooh-arr, there could be no doubt that some top-level looting and pillaging was about to hit the deck, and the cabin boy had better down that tankard of rum to prepare himself for a thorough rogering.

Warwick from Enniskillen*: What did Jesus do with the presents that the Three Wise Men gave him? Did he just dump them up in the attic with all his other crap presents, or did he go and trade them in at Game for an Xbox or something?*

Jesus did not care a jot about his gold, frankincense and myrrh; like all babies, he was only interested in the packaging.

Dan in Melbourne*: Where does the term 'boot camp' come from? I can't imagine running in boots would be good for blisters.*

That's enough outta you, maggot! You get your answers from us, and you leave your goddamn *imagination* at home with your apple-pie girlfriend. FIFTY PRESS-UPS! While you're doin' that, sizzle-dick, we'll be jaw-bonin' the truth about the phrase 'boot camp', which actually has nothing to do with boots. Weird, huh? CAN'T HEAR YOU, PUSSY. That's right. Weird.

The 'boot' half of the term is apparently a reference to sailors' leggings during the Spanish-American War, which were known colloquially as boots. YESSIR. LEGGINGS. Somethin' funny, Rambo? Let's see how hard you laugh when you do FIFTY MORE PRESS-UPS AND LICK THE FLOOR!

Maybe your tiny little worm-brain concludes from all this that there must have been camps training these sailors to wear these leggings, which then became known as 'boot camps'. WRONG! Toffs don't refer to Cheltenham Ladies' College as 'Pashmina Camp', do they? DO THEY? No, they don't, Tinkerbell. What actually happened is that many years later, by the time the US Army was training their personnel en masse in residential centres, 'boot' was well-established slang for 'recruit', even though leggings were no longer worn. NOW QUIT ASKING QUESTIONS, or we may have to get all Accidental Discharge on your ass, and we AIN'T talking love juice. Fudgepacker.

Andrew from Northamptonshire: Why is Boxing Day called Boxing Day?

When one spends a full day with one's family gorging on trans-fats in front of *Ant and Dec's Top 10 Christmas Blunders*, domestic disagreements are bound to flare up; but, surprisingly, the origins of this festival have nowt to do with fisticuffs. In fact, it might as well be called 'Boxes Day', because it derives from the tradition of rich folk handing out boxes of presents to their servants the day after Christmas. Some churches even had a big box into which the congregation put presents for the poor, much as nowadays BHS celebrates the season with a bargain bin of cut-price scatter cushions.

Boxing Day is also the feast day of St Stephen, patron saint of cold turkey sandwiches, who was ordained specifically to supervise the distribution of alms from the church coffers. So it is probably in tribute to him that, centuries later, benevolence became associated with 26 December . You remember the barn-storming carol 'Good King Wenceslas': the King wakes up, on the feast of Stephen, with a stinking hangover. He opens his curtains

? to admire the snow, deep and crisp and even, and instead spies a peasant nicking logs off his estate. Does he unleash the hounds? No. Does he make him compete in a bumfight with the tramp who sits outside Londis? No. Not on St Stephen's Day. Instead he commands his page to trek with him through the snow to the peasant's faraway hovel, to deliver him a load of meat, booze and firewood. And every Boxing Day we think of this heartwarming tale when Uncle Ken storms out of the living room halfway through an overheated game of Risk.

Polly from Trowbridge: What purpose did the horns on Viking helmets serve?

We can think of three obvious purposes:

1. hooks for flower-baskets
2. punching holes in stubborn jam-jar lids
3. signal-boosters for Harald Hardrada's wifi router.

Despite this, the only genuine Viking helmet so far unearthed by archaeologists possessed a grand total of ZERO HORNS, and the whole horny-headed Vikings image is believed to be a total fabrication. Most common-or-garden Vikings would have sported neat leather caps, because wearing a big metal bowl on their heads would severely impede their ability to run around the battlefield conking Saxons on the noggin with axes. Additional horns would provide a useful handle for enemies, get stuck in trees, hamper their aerodynamics, and generally be quite hard to take seriously.

But, feeling that caps didn't make their Viking forebears appear threatening and pointy enough, apparently the nineteenth-century Swedes came up with the now-stereotypical depiction. Their inspiration may have been ancient ceremonial headgear which was decorated with dramatic protuberances, rather like

Bronze Age Tellytubby-heads. Or maybe they saw Otto von Bismarck yomping around Europe in his single-spiked hat and thought they could double the fun.

> **If, in 1000 years' time, we find ourselves writing a misleading history book, what would we stick on top of Our Boys' helmets?**
>
> 1 egg whisks
> 2 pez dispensers
> 3 bird table
> 4 a full-size maypole
> 5 giant foam finger

Alex: Why do shops offering key-cutting services invariably also offer shoe repair?

Under the guise of getting spare keys for the back gate, we actually went and got the answer from a bonafide key-cutting shoe-repairer. And here's news for you, Alex: shoe repair was originally the star of the show, and key-cutting the Eve Harrington of the world of cobblers. In days of yore, when a pair of shoes was expected to last at least as long as the average human life, one would take them to be resoled periodically to keep the cholera-laced puddlewater out of one's socks.

Then in the late 1970s/early 1980s (our source wasn't too exact on this point, choking with emotion at the memory of when it all started to go wrong for him and his ilk), bargain shoe-shops began springing up all over the place, meaning that rather than keeping their footwear going for future generations, people would just buy a new pair. Even if they didn't need one! Times became hard for the professional shoe-resoler, because hardly anyone was inclined to pay to resole a plastic shoe that only cost them £10 to start with.

Rather than go the way of the crinoline-architect or periwig-fluffer, plucky cobblers realised they must adapt to survive, and began sniffing around for extra services they could offer to bolster the ailing sole business, rather like when Chessington World of Adventures, née Zoo, calculated that punters would pay far more to 'ride the Vampire' than look at llamas.

Alongside the occasional diversion into passport photobooths, luggage tags, Swiss Army knives and watch batteries, almost all high-street cobblers plumped for key cutting. Not just because it's a safe money-spinner – people always seem to enjoy keeping their houses locked – but also key-cutting machinery is not too bulky, so they could easily find room for it alongside the shoe rehabilitation equipment.

And with that, the friendly chap straightened up, wiped his misty eyes, and inhaled a deep lungful of shoe-repair solvents to prepare himself for the inevitable day when swipe-card locks and fingerprint recognition force him to add a dog-grooming counter atop his display case of wallets.

Lola from Leamington Spa: What is the origin of 'diaper' as the transatlantic word for 'nappy'?

It derives from the Old French word 'diapre', which meant a white silken damask-like cloth. Evidently those transatlantic nappies are a posher affair than our humble British shit-absorbers.

Helen says:

My nappies were certainly not made of damask. They were in fact made of sandpaper-rough greyish towelling. And how do I know this? Because my mother has STILL GOT THEM! If you don't think this is weird, bear in mind the woman last had a baby in 1980.

To her credit, these ghastly rags served all three of the Zaltzman brats and are still going strong today as dusters, which means she should probably receive some kind of a prize from Greenpeace for being the Home Counties' most assiduous recycler. But seeing her wiping down the kitchen counters with a decommissioned crap-sack really kills off one's appetite for lunch.

Vincenzo: Where's the pride in London Pride?

The beer 'London Pride', to which we assume Vincenzo refers, is in fact named after a perennial flowering hybrid of Spanish Pyrenees and Irish saxifrages (stop us if you've heard this before, Titchmarsh). The plant is known for its propensity to grow upon inhospitable terrain – e.g. the rubble of bombed-out houses during the Blitz – so it came to symbolise the Irrepressible Spirit of Plucky Londoners, Gawd Bless 'Em.

War-related beer names, like Bombardier, Courage and Spitfire, have always perplexed us a bit. Sure, in today's cynical nation it can be stirring to see a little patriotic display; but, when we're sinking a refreshing pint, we'd rather not be reminded of a devastating six-year conflict, thanks very much. Is the foaming ale coursing

? down our throats really the most fitting tribute to the war dead? Is the derring-do resilience of our forefathers best summed up by a drink that *isn't even fizzy*?

If you answered 'yes' to the above, and you work for a booze company, do us a favour and please discount the following names for any future battle-beers:

Bang!
Dawn Raid
Powdered Egg
Black Market Nylons
Do You Remember Bananas?
We Slept In Balham Tube Station
Death of the Youth of a Nation
Goodbye, Grandma

David: I do tours up and down the Thames and I tell people regularly that 'wharf' stands for 'WareHouse At River Front'. I'm pretty sure I made that up; but does it have any historical grounding at all?

Here's a truism, readers, which you could use as an emergency goldfish bowl because it really holds water:

Whenever someone claims that a word came from an acronym, they are almost certainly bullshitting.*

You certainly are, David. No, you did not inadvertently coincide with etymological fact. 'Wharf' actually comes from the late Old English word 'hwearf', which meant 'shipyard' or 'water's edge'. Feel free to continue fibbing to tourists though; it's one of the few sports we actually enjoy.

* unless they are referring to 'laser' or 'radar'

Past Times

Laura and Tom: You know how computers used to be cream, but now they're always black, white or silver? Will they ever go back to being cream? This might seem a trivial question, but we just had an argument with our dad about it.

Younger readers might not even remember the drab monotony which reigned supreme in the world of IT before Apple brought out that range of snazzy iMacs that looked like blue and orange crash-helmets. But yes, through the twentieth century, beige was the colour of choice for the PC, because the mere notion of computers in everyday life was still so thrillingly space-age that they had to keep them as subdued-looking as possible, lest people's internal organs liquefied with excitement.

Beige is nobody's favourite colour (and if it is, we do not want to be your friend) so we can't see any persuasive reason for it to make a mass comeback in the computer market. But it would be highly foolish to write it off; plenty other incomprehensible revivals have happened. We're looking at *you*, mullets, high-waisted jeans, and Shaggy.

It saddens us that such an inconsequential matter has caused a falling-out between you and your father. It's so often the silly things, isn't it, that cause the decades-long rifts in families. And trust us, this *will* look like a silly thing when in twenty years you're trying to explain to your kids why they've never met their granddad. Let computers be all the colours of the rainbow, Laura and Tom – family's too important.

Matthew from Colchester: I can't think of any gay ghosts or black ghosts. Is the spirit world homophobic and racist?

The spirit world is an unlikely place to find forward thinking of any sort, and amongst the generations of racists and homophobes who now float around castle corridors, looking all translucent and going 'wooooo', discriminatory attitudes die hard. But there's no reason to assume that black and gay ghosts don't exist, insofar as any ghost could be said to exist (anyone claiming to have actually seen one is categorically talking a load of arse). Most of the ghosts Matthew is likely to run into around Colchester will be dead Brits from Days of Yore – and the population of Yore tended to be Caucasian and closeted.

Sexual preference is hard to determine thanks to the fey demeanour inherent in a lot of ghostly behaviour: ruffs, tights and an inclination towards melodrama seem to go with the territory.* But a ghost we're certain is a Scream Queen is the one who is said to frequent the Theatre Royal, Drury Lane. To endure five years of *My Fair Lady*, and then still hang around for a decade of *Miss Saigon* and *The Producers*: these are simply not the actions of a heterosexual man, dead or alive.

Furthermore, it is hard to ascertain the colour of a ghost's skin when said skin is spectrally transparent, or covered in a shroud. But, unlike Matthew from Colchester, we can think of a black ghost: Candyman, the claw-handed African-American spookster of the book and film of the same name. Following a terrible life in which he is enslaved, mutilated by plantation owners, and killed by a swarm of bees, he hangs around for centuries, haunting people's bathroom mirrors wearing a pimp jacket and shouting 'Boo!' before splashing gore everywhere. To summon him, one need only look in a mirror and say 'Candyman' five times out loud. It's pretty terrifying the first time, but as with all horror movie monsters, the more you see him, the less scary he becomes. Nowadays we invoke him just to help us with our admin.

---

* Furthermore, all ghosts channelled by Derek Acorah will sound gay, whether they are or not.

Aled in Pontypridd: Piggy banks, what's the deal with them? Where did this tradition of putting pennies in pigs come from? Who was insane enough to think of that? I mean, this guy could have thought of something much cuter, like a penguin or something, but instead he chose a fucking pig!!!

Mystery shrouds the identity of the precise individual who first manufactured a clay pig and stuck their loose change, foreign currency and laundry tokens into it. But you may as well choose a favourite character from *The Canterbury Tales* and pretend it was them, because the origins of the term 'piggy bank' go all the way back to ye olden times, maketh no mistaeke.

The Middle English word 'pygg' denoted a sturdy clay used to make 'pygg jars' to keep cash in. By the eighteenth century, 'pygg' became 'pig' and it became popular for the jars to be shaped like pigs to fit their name. Which was convenient, because making a giraffe out of clay is rather more difficult.

Daniel from Borehamwood: Why do people throw bottles at ships on their maiden voyages?

Because a lot of drunks sleep on piers. But the origins of this tradition go way back to ancient times, when a goat would be sacrificed and its blood smeared over the front of a ship to ensure good luck for the crew.* Then the Greeks got into wine, and over time the tradition was adapted so that alcohol was used to toast the ship rather than blood. It may seem wasteful, but it's a more positive omen than having some freshly squeezed animal matter dripping off the front of your ship.

* . . . and pretty shitty luck for the goat.

Louise from Scotland: What did the very first email ever say?

The first ever email was sent in 1971 by Ray Tomlinson, an engineer at computer company Bolt, Beranek and Newman in Cambridge, Massachusetts. So excited was he by his technological achievement – getting two computers to exchange a message using the @ sign to determine location – that he didn't put a great deal of imagination into the content itself. The message simply said: 'QWERTYUIOP'. Snore! No wonder it took another two decades for email to catch on.

Daniel from Preston: Why are ladybirds called 'lady' birds? Can they not be both sexes? Surely half of them should be called 'man' birds, or would this just lead to more confusion as this is a direct contradiction?

Ladybirds are a very feminist strain of insect. They see your linguistic patriarchy, Daniel from Preston, and they're going to take it down, one back garden at a time. For the record, male ladybirds are *totally* comfortable with being called ladybirds; and, unlike most blokes, they're also completely happy to be seen in public wearing polka dots.

You're right to point out, though, that thinking literally about the word 'ladybird' is the fast track to a world of confusion. To the Sixties generation, it's a tautology; to the rest of us it conjures up a mental picture of Doris Day crossed with a falcon.

To make sense of it we must go back in time, to the Middle Ages, when devastated farmers saw their crops destroyed by aphids and other pests. When they saw these spotted little beasts flying in, gobbling up the aphids and saving the day, the relieved farmers cried, 'Hail Mary!' and named their insect saviours 'Our Lady's Birds' in tribute to her, the most ladylike lady of all. Then they realised that by the time one had managed to say excitedly to one's companions, 'Ooh, look, one of Our Lady's Birds has just landed on my finger!' it had already flown off, so over time this contracted to 'ladybird'.

You might think it pretty silly that they got called 'birds' at all when there's not a feather or beak on them, but even more inappropriately, in many Slavonic languages their name translates to 'God's little cow'. They don't moo. They don't stand around in fields. You can't even milk them (we've rarely felt so disappointed). That, Daniel, should keep your philological indignation in perspective.

Adrienne: How did people wake up before the alarm clock was invented?

There are myriad inventions which we shudder to imagine life without: fridges, sewerage systems, anaesthesia . . . How on earth did people struggle through life without Slankets? Or McFlurries? Or penguin-shaped shower radios? In a world before you could watch Justin Bieber videos on your iPhone, was it even worth waking up at all?

Apparently so, because before alarm clocks you might have been woken by the crow of cockerels, the sun, the town crier, the bong of church bells, or by the thud of another family member dropping dead from typhus.

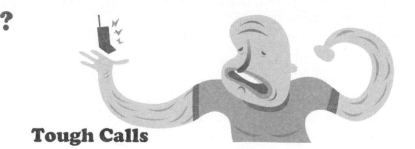

Tough Calls

Which would you rather have sex with, a rock or a hard place? It's that sort of thing in this section, plus moral dilemmas and other tricky brainteasers – because if you can't make your own vital decisions, it's sensible to refer them to us and wait a few years for us to respond in a book.

Spoonhead from Lincoln: My wife and I had to make a large decision recently, whether to get a spaniel or have a baby. The baby won through in the end, and some months later out she was pulled, kicking, screaming and bloody. So answer me this: how soon should I start training her to act as a gun dog? Is six months too soon?

Here, Spoonhead, you have highlighted the inherent deficiencies of young mankind when compared to young dogkind. Granted, the lifespan of the average dog is about one sixth that of the average Western human, but developmentally, dogs are much quicker out of the gate. Observe the comparative study opposite.

Cheer up, though: your choice of heir over hound does have quite a few benefits. All going according to plan, Little Spoonhead can look after you when you're old and decrepit, long after the Spoonhound would have perished. Spoonchild probably won't sit drooling underneath the dinner table at every meal, or dig a series of holes in your lawn, or eat a box of Ferrero Rocher whole then puke up gold foil all around the house. She

AGE	DOG	HUMAN
1 day	Quite cute. Makes you laugh with its tiny pratfalls and funny little face	Looks like a tiny scarlet screaming old man. Makes you cry, not because you're overcome with emotion, but because you can't believe you've produced such a foul creature
1 month	Can walk	Can't even walk
3 months	Snoozes on the sofa all day	Keeps you awake all night
6 months	Can roll over, pretend to dance on hind legs, and catch a stick mid-air	Can roll over, just about
1 year	Semi-operational gundog	Can chew on the corner of a book
4 years	Retrieves hundreds of dead pheasants from your country estate	Gives you nightmares about which school to send them to
7 years	Scared a burglar away from your house	Shoplifted a Milky Way from the corner shop
10 years	Too old and lazy to fetch your pipe and slippers	Can use your computer far better and quicker than you can, or ever will
13 years	Bit smelly	Bit smelly
14 years	Dead	You wish they were dead

is unlikely to lick her anus in polite company, unless she takes a decidedly racy career path.

But face it: she's never going to win you any prizes at Crufts.

James from Gloucestershire: *I'm 17 and I have a 43-year-old neighbour who wants to sleep with me. She's fit and I would quite happily dick her, but she's my mum's friend and has a scary husband. Am I right to be cautious? Should I just man up and do the job?*

Let's just ponder this for a minute. Erm . . . OF COURSE NOT! ARE YOU QUITE INSANE? Much as this scenario would make for a decent coming-of-age indie drama or French film, in real life it is fraught with problems. Firstly, the moral misdemeanour of knowingly destroying someone's marriage: we're aware that morals are not too bothersome for a tumescent 17-year-old, but if you can think with your brain rather than your wang for a sec, you will agree it's really not polite.

Secondly: don't piss off your neighbours. Decades-long street wars have been triggered by a wrongly placed wheelie bin, so imagine the potential devastation to be wrought by the already-scary husband if and when he were to discover the cuckoldry. He can pop round to knock your block off and be back on his sofa before the end of the ad break. Or, worse still, he might ask to join in.

Thirdly, are you prepared for the fact that *your mum* will know all about your sordid affairs? Her next coffee-and-gossip session with her friend could leave her needing years of Freudian therapy. Even if she can handle a frank account of her special little boy in a *Graduate*-esque shagfest (and if she can, YUK), she will store it in her nagging arsenal for the rest of her natural life. Offset the minutes of pleasure now with the knowledge that at her eightieth birthday party, she *will* bring it up in front of everyone as revenge when you accidentally leave a ring mark on the coffee table.

In the name of all that is prudent, quell this fire in your loins, promise yourself not to bone anyone who doesn't live at least two streets away, and if your neighbour asks you to pop over to her house for a minute 'to help move some furniture', JUST SAY NO.

Jason in Colchester: An ex-colleague has offered me £100 to write the financial paper for her Leisure and Entertainment university degree. Should I do it?

Olly says:

YES! Conscience be damned: your friend is being resourceful, recognising the limits of her own abilities and using her network of contacts to achieve business goals – her professors would be proud. Outsourcing is a growth industry, and she's leading from the front. If her starting offer is £100, you can probably haggle her up to £150. There are no losers here! Unless you know nothing about finance, in which case she'll learn a valuable lesson in choosing her suppliers more carefully.

NO! That's academic fraud. She won't learn anything if you write her paper for her, and together you're making a mockery of Leisure and Entertainment degrees. Which is really kicking a dog when it's down.

Helen says:

Anna: A log flume has been erected at the end of my road. Is it wrong to really really want to have a go? I am 30 in six months' time.

'Is it wrong?' What are you, a nun? You have the option to go for a ride in a fake hollowed-out LOG! Along a man-made stream! At a 45-degree gradient! Why on earth would anyone *not* want to go on it?

Olly says: A log flume ride was THE highlight of our school French Exchange. (Other memorable bits: Danny Glover's dubbed voice in *Lethal Weapon 3*; pretending to enjoy pork for the fourth consecutive dinner with my gentile Exchange family; avoiding the girl I fancied in case eye contact exposed my lascivious inner monologue.) The Flume concerned was in the 'Walibi Schtroumpf' park in Metz, then meticulously themed to resemble a village from *The Smurfs.**

A couple of mates and I were on the Smurfy Smurf Log Flume, about to head up Smurf Hill, when our log began to fill up with water. Luckily the staff noticed, and paused the ride. Before we had time to panic, three grumpy, sweaty French maintenance men WEARING SMURF HATS turned up and bailed out our log with buckets, without saying a word. Then, as if we'd dreamt the whole thing, the ride started up ▶

* It has since undergone some sort of ethnic cleansing programme in which its Smurfiness has been stripped away and replaced with Wild West and Transylvania clichés. Papa Smurf will return one day and they will feel his Smurfy wrath.

again, and off we floated, paralysed with fear that we would meet our deaths in the waterways of Smurfsville. If only my pocket money had stretched to purchasing the photo that was taken as we plunged down the final canyon! A print-out of my face, contorted in pure terror: I can't imagine a more apt keepsake of my French Exchange experience. ∎

Kirsty: Would you rather pubes for teeth, or teeth for pubes?

Let's weigh up the consequences of this genito-dental dilemma:

	PROS	CONS
Pubes for teeth	Self-flossing	You've got a mouthful of pubes
	Festive – dye them different colours for parties and religious holidays	Think on it – your mouth would be FULL of PUBES
	No need for braces – just use hair-straighteners!	PUBES! FILLING YOUR MOUTH!
Teeth for pubes	Educational new perspective on fellatio – FINALLY see how it looks from inside your partner's mouth	Sexy fun with chocolate body paint? No thanks; think of all the fillings you'd need
	Those crabs ain't got nowhere to hide	Risk of biting your own knob whilst jogging
	Minty-fresh crotch	Already tiresome and painful, dental appointments would take on a whole new dimension of humiliation

There's little contest. Wang-fangs win the day: a permanent mouthful of pubes is the sort of prospect that wakes us in the night screaming, sweating and reaching for the Gillette.

Dave: My best friend, the man I want to ask to be my best man, in the past had a sexual interaction with my fiancée. Now my fiancée thinks this is a little weird. What should I do?

Regardless of what you think is right, you must DO AS YOUR BRIDE TELLS YOU. It is HER day. You and your wedding-day wishes and needs are purely incidental; all you are responsible for is turning up, saying 'I do', and smiling in the photographs. You're worried your best friend will be pissed off at you for a while? You're signing a contract to be married to this woman FOREVER. Vex her on your wedding day and you will pay and pay and pay for the rest of your life, and if there's an afterlife, you'll be paying there as well.

Besides, her feelings of weirdness are not completely unreasonable. Perhaps she fears that your friend would make a particularly blue best man's speech. Perhaps she does not want to be a blushing bride in the sense of blushing at the thought of a three-way at the altar. Perhaps she has watched too many romantic comedies and fears that your friend will shout, 'I object!', pick her up in his arms and run down the aisle outside into a smug sexy ever-after, leaving you, Dave, wrecked in front of all your family and friends and with no date to accompany you to the reception for which you've shelled out your year's net income.

So if you value your own happiness, demote your best friend to chief usher or something, and choose as your best man someone from your group of friends or close relations with whom your wife-elect has not had sexual contact. Assuming there remains such a person; if not, you might need to rethink the marriage entirely.

Walter from LA: I live in Los Angeles and am not in any way part of, or desire to be a part of, the entertainment industry. Given that, why in the hell do I live here? It's damn expensive! I don't go to clubs, and my friends are basically fine, but I think I could do better. What do you think?

We think:

1. You have no wish to be a pedestrian.
2. You like to live within easy reach of several theme-parks.
3. Weird plastic surgery gives you the giggles.
4. You still get a kick out of the possibility of running into Courteney Cox at the petrol station.
5. You actually *enjoy* the fact that you're over LA – as thousands flock there with dreams of making it big, you smirk happily, knowing that you're not one of those idiots whose dreams are 99.9999 per cent likely to be crushed. It's cooler not to care, right? But . . .
6. . . . You nonetheless secretly harbour a hope that one day, as you queue to pay for your soy chai latte, you will be Discovered.

Jack from Stoke: I am feeling guilty. I am a killer. A rabbit killer. I was in my garden, bored, and I tried to make my sister's rabbits go into a cage like a sheepdog would do. However I managed to scare them out of the garden. I was then met with sounds of barking dogs and rustling of trees. To my relief, one of the rabbits came back; I waited for the other but it didn't come. I just went inside and forgot about it. After being out I came home to find my sister crying that her rabbit had been broken to death by this dog. I haven't said it was me.

? *I CAN'T. So answer me this please: what do I do in this situation? Do I say I had nothing to do with it and then tell her when she's 20 and probably doesn't give a toss, or admit to my mistakes?*

We've always considered ourselves very moral, straight-up, truth-is-always-best people.

Not this time.

Swallow that guilt, Jack from Stoke, and DO NOT FESS UP. What possible good will come of it? We'll tell you: none! Blurting out the truth won't bring poor Flopsy back. It might salve your conscience for a microsecond, before your sister/parents/the RSPCA release a parade of retribution that lasts far, far longer than that rabbit would have done had it not become dog-food.

You could buy her a new rabbit, but be sure to do so in a way that suggests you are merely playing the Thoughtful Brother card and not overcompensating for your complicity in an act of lapinicide.

Barrie the tinytrucker: *Which is better, cremation or burial?*

If Barrie were referring to the dubstep recording artist Burial, we could straightforwardly answer 'cremation'. As it is, there are some crucial factors to be considered before deciding which method of corpse-clearance is quantifiably 'better':

1. The Ceremony

Being dropped into a hole and having a load of earth shovelled on top of you is properly, unambiguously conclusive. In comparison, cremations seem less authentic – for a start, the coffin's on a conveyer belt, making your final send-off redolent of lunch at Yo! Sushi. Even the recipients of the ashes feel doubts: is this *really* 100 per cent Grandad?

Open-air cremations, still practised in some countries, are pretty cool. But a burning pyre just doesn't look right on the towpath of the Droitwich Canal. So, burial has the edge here.

Burial   💀💀💀💀💀💀💀🩶🩶🩶
Cremation   💀💀💀💀💀💀💀🩶🩶🩶

2. Environment

Why buy energy-saving lightbulbs to compensate for your annual fly-drive holidays if you then employ a huge emissions-spewing barbecue to rid the world of your carcass? Burial wastes less energy, unless you're one of those fifty-stone fatties who needs to be lowered into your grave by crane; you can choose a renewably-sourced biodegradable wicker coffin; plus you posthumously enrich the ecosystem when a family of worms feasts upon your eyeballs.

Burial   💀💀💀💀💀💀💀🩶🩶🩶
Cremation   💀💀💀💀💀💀🩶🩶🩶🩶

3. Taphephobia[1] vs. Pyrophobia[2]

It's highly unlikely you'll wake up inside your coffin, but Helen has commissioned one with a Sudoku inside the lid just in case. Being trapped deep underground, slowly losing oxygen and unable to summon the energy to escape . . . it's a hellish prospect, which is why we avoid the Tube in rush hour.

Being cremated alive is also far from ideal, but at least the shock and fumes mean you'd pass out pretty quickly, and even if your flame-licked body were to burst out of the oven for one final lap, it would make for a memorable swansong.

Burial   💀🩶🩶🩶🩶🩶🩶🩶🩶🩶
Cremation   💀💀💀🩶🩶🩶🩶🩶🩶🩶

[1] The surprisingly widespread fear of being buried alive.
[2] The pretty rational fear of being burnt alive.

4. Final Resting Place

If you're buried, your final resting place is pretty damned final, barring landslides, meteor strikes or the excavations of unscrupulous property developers. Reassuring, yes; but who needs comfort when you can have *fun*? Cremation leaves you more portable than you've been since you were a baby, so the range of options is far broader. Your family can keep you on the mantelpiece, as a morbid conversation piece. They can pack your remains into a firework and set you off in one last cathartic dazzle. They can scatter you in one of your favourite scenic spots, or back into their own faces if there's a strong wind blowing that day. They can respond to one of those unconvincing-looking adverts in the weekend colour supplements and have you made into a diamond. They can mix you up with some plaster of Paris and make you into a doorstop. They can make like Keith Richards and chop you into lines and snort you. They can sprinkle you on their breakfast cereal. They can even chuck you in the bin, because they never liked you much.

Burial 💀💀💀 ⚪⚪⚪⚪⚪⚪⚪

Cremation 💀💀💀💀💀💀💀💀💀 ⚪

5. Exhumation

You've only just been laid to rest, and now they suspect your passing was hastened by foul play! The police disinter your coffin and run toxicology tests on your putrefying corpse. If, instead, you were cremated and sprinkled around the roots of a tree in the forest you loved, they haven't a hope of finding you. Even if they've got your full urn, what are they going to do – add water and mix you to a paste in the hope it'll reanimate you? Sadly not. Case dismissed for lack of forensic evidence.

Burial 💀💀💀💀💀💀💀 ⚪⚪⚪

Cremation 💀💀💀💀💀💀💀💀💀💀

Final Score
Burial: 25 out of 50
Cremation: 25 out of 50

Conclusion
Our careful calculations show that burial and cremation are much of a muchness, although neither is especially nice, because they both involve being dead. In conclusion, Barrie, the best of both worlds is to be cremated, and then have your ashes scattered into a coffin and buried.

Rebecca from London: My boyfriend, who is lovely and perfect in most respects, has pictures of scantily clad women on his walls which I really don't like. We've been together for a couple of months and I've never said anything about them; how do I make him get rid of them without embarrassing him?

Glue little paper raincoats over them. Your boyfriend will either be moved to get rid of them or of you. At least you will know where his loyalties lie.

Harvey: My girlfriend is thinking of buying a Citroën Pluriel. Olly, answer me this: what are the drawbacks of this piece of shit car?

Harvey is being provocative, because as he well knows, Olly has been the proud owner of a baby blue and NOT AT ALL designed for girls Citroën Pluriel since September 2005. This is the Mann rundown of Pluriel pros and cons for Harvey and his girlfriend to consider:

PLURIEL FEATURE	PROS	CONS
6-CD changer	No need to go through the hassle of manually ejecting a CD: with a flick of the wrist, you can change discs using buttons on the steering wheel	Risk of distractedly swerving into oncoming traffic You still use CDs, Grandad? You look like a twat
'Surf-style' Folding Tailgate	Sit on your fold-out boot and eat your sandwiches whilst gazing at the ocean. Or the car park at KFC. Whichever is closer	You are not a surfer You are sitting IN A CAR BOOT You look like a twat
Full-length canvas roof	It's a convertible, it's a cabriolet, it's a tiny pick-up truck! You choose	Sunburn Leaks You look like a twat
A range of colours	Black, red and grey are so boring! Choose your weapon: fluorescent orange, baby blue which is IN NO WAY designed for girls, or lime green	Can cause blindness in other road users Falling bird shit results in weird 'tie-dye' effect You look like a twat

Sophie: If you had a choice, would you rather look like a fish or smell like a fish?

Fish don't really pong until they die, so we'd rather smell a bit like a fish than be forced to live the rest of our lives in a freakshow, undergoing medical testing, or on *Oprah*. Providing we conducted all our social arrangements and business meetings in branches of Livebait, no one would even notice.

Tough Calls

Dan: Who would win in a fight between the Grim Reaper and King Midas?

Presumably the Grim Reaper would try to avoid hand-to-hand combat, and, upon attempting to grimly reap Midas, his legendary scythe would turn to gold on contact. Gold is quite a soft metal, not ideal for functional scythe blades, but even a soft blunt scythe can still do some damage. Either way, Midas is in for quite a thumping.

His Grimness would of course be in trouble if Midas gets a decent hold on him, but the odds are slim, for the gilded monarch will definitely be in sub-optimal fighting condition. Midas's choice of divine gifts means that anything which touches his lips turns to gold – including water and protein shakes. Therefore only a couple of days after receiving his compulsory begolding ability, Midas would be in a severely weakened state; in a few more days, he would be dead of dehydration and starvation. Victory by default to the Reaper.

Fred and Kane from Kent: We read that convicts on Death Row get free healthcare. If a guy that was about to die in the electric chair had a heart attack, would they save him?

It does seem a bit silly to save someone from dying naturally just so that they can pay to kill him, but yes, they would. Imagine, Fred and Kane from Kent, that you're in charge of Death Row. You've spent millions of dollars keeping Mr Naughty in prison while his appeals process rumbles on for a decade or more. So when the time finally comes that you're allowed to despatch him from society, are you really going to let a little thing like Natural Causes prevent you from FRYING THE BASTARD? No, you wouldn't, because if you'd taken a job like Head of Death Row in

? the first place, you probably believe in vengeance, an eye for an eye, two wrongs making a right, and other things of which Jesus Christ would not approve.

Jacquelyne: If I were elected Prime Minister, my first act would be to pass a law banning men over 30 and all men with beer bellies from wearing Speedos in public. Especially men with beer bellies so big that they hang down so far over the front that you can't tell if they are actually wearing anything at all. If you had the power to pass any law concerning items of clothing that should or shouldn't be worn, what would it be and why?

You'll never get that law passed, Jacquelyne, if you're elected Prime Minister of France: in many French swimming pools, men are actually bound by law to wear Speedos rather than more capacious trunks. They claim this is for reasons of hygiene, but we suspect it's really because, following the Revolution and the subsequent decades of unrest, they just want to feel sure that *some* things in life will remain orderly.

It is remarkable that gents with the physiques of snowmen happily parade around in nowt more than a banana hammock and a sunhat, whilst their far trimmer wives and girlfriends would rather be seen in a burqa than a bikini. But aren't these chaps simply exhibiting the body-fascist-defying confidence that Gok Wan insists we all espouse? Rather than averting our eyes from these gutsy (in all senses) fellows, perhaps we should in fact worship them as paragons of Learning To Love Yourself, Despite Visual Evidence To The Contrary.

The men who so offend Jacquelyne are making the best of an impossible situation, because on the face of the Earth there is not one single item of swimwear that flatters a paunch. The sartorial choices we would choose to ban (see opposite) are, in

HELEN AND OLLY'S SARTORIAL SHITLIST

- High heels on the under-10s: if you're too young to read *Lolita*, you're too young to dress like her. Also, in the long term, a podiatry nightmare.
- Jeans which you buy pre-trashed and splattered with paint: help your auntie renovate her bathroom to achieve the same effect on a budget.
- People who wear tracksuits ALL DAY: in our experience, they are either breeders of fighting dogs, or have given up on life.
- Ultra-low-slung trousers, as sported by teenage boys: if your buttocks get wet when you sit on a bench, your trousers AREN'T WORKING.
- Kanye West-style slatted sunglasses: they make *him* look like a knob-end, and he's a popstar. *You* just look like a wannabe knob-end.
- Men's pinstriped shirts with flowers embroidered on: 'I'm all business, but with a soft side. Oh, who am I kidding – I'm just a tit.'
- Uggs.

our opinion, indicative of a flawed character. Yes, we do judge by appearance. Yes, we are shallow.

Si from Takeley: My mate Strongy claims to have seen porn in which a person (can't remember if he said man or woman) has an entire pineapple shoved up their arse! Assuming that this is possible, answer me this: if you had to have a whole pineapple shoved up your arse,

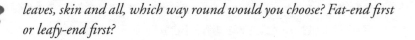

leaves, skin and all, which way round would you choose? Fat-end first or leafy-end first?

Shoved? We'd prefer lubricated and gently glided in, if we must submit to this assault at all. Naturally we would choose fat-end first: if you insist we must suffer excruciating pain for a brief period before anally bleeding to death, we might as well have a pretty sprig of leaves trailing out our backsides. What fun we'd have, pretending to be chorus girls in an unusually gruesome production of *Copacabana*.

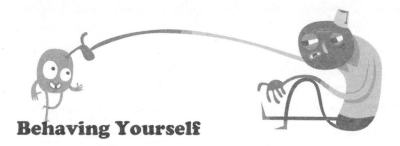

Behaving Yourself

For those of you who didn't attend etiquette school in your gap year, modern manners can be a minefield. Heed our advice herein and you won't make a tit of yourself at work, offend the in-laws or be blacklisted by your so-called friends.

Luke: How can one achieve respectability with the minimum of fuss?

Sport a bowler hat, moustache and smart suit. Accessorise with a proper umbrella (not a fold-up one!), a briefcase, and a rolled-up copy of the *London Review of Books* tucked under your arm. Even if you had a dead baby and some anal beads hanging out of your pocket, nobody would raise an eyebrow.

Ali from London: How can I stop my boyfriend picking his nose? He doesn't do it in public, but saves up all his picking for when we're at home together. Any suggestions?

Three words: sexual reward system.

Josie: My mother sends me things constantly in the post which are inappropriate – for example CDs of Danielle Steele adaptations from the Daily Mail. *How can I tactfully explain that I never want to receive another* Daily Mail *package in my entire life?*

Move house, and don't tell her your new address.

Tommy from Ely: Should brothers and sisters be allowed to marry? Obviously they shouldn't really have children, but if they're not hurting anyone and are consenting adults, should other people feeling icky about it stop them from getting together?

We're not sure what would motivate amorous siblings to get hitched in the first place. They've already got the same surname. They're already each other's next of kin. If it's approval in the eyes of God they're seeking, well, He did turn a blind eye to Adam and Eve's kids pairing off with each other; but in recent years He's taken *ages* to decide about female priests and homosexuality, so He probably won't get round to reviewing His incest policy for yonks.

We do identify some hypocrisy around this taboo. No doubt there are many people who bash the bishop to *Bouncy Lesbian Twins III* and yet, without any hint of irony, fume at the thought of heterosexual siblings getting it on. But the status quo is still for the best. Let's face it, marriage was established first and foremost for the purposes of procreation, and it's natural for civilised societies to steer clear of endorsing any distortions to the gene pool. It would be pretty tricky to enshrine in law inexact Tommy's stipulation that brothers and sisters 'shouldn't really have children' – and how would it be enforced, with an elite squad of child-catchers? Even if it were legally and biologically excusable for siblings to breed, the children would suffer at Christmas: one combined set of grandparents equals half the number of book tokens.

Brendan from Hinckley in Leicestershire: I've just woken up and realised I've slept through my alarm clock. What's the best excuse for being late to work?

You could try telling the unembroidered, unvarnished truth, but this method should only be wheeled out if your boss is the kind of person who would respond to the statement, 'Yup, I slept in,' by clapping you on the shoulder and barking, 'I *like* you, Brendan! You say what you think. I like that. What the heck, I'm giving you a promotion!' However, this only happens in sitcoms, so it's a risky tactic.

Even when you are genuinely late for work because your alarm failed you, or the dog ate your bus pass, or your train was stuck just outside the station for two hours whilst staff tried to coax a suicidal commuter off the tracks, your boss *will not believe you.* Nor will they care to listen to your contrition-laced account of your morning ordeal, which you've probably laced with lots of details to make it sound extra convincing even though that makes everyone more suspicious that you're fibbing.

You might be able to joke your way out of trouble, because any decent boss will prefer a well-crafted, entertaining fiction to a tedious truth. And if yours doesn't, you might as well have fun before you're sent to clear your desk. So don't trifle with your run-of-the-mill excuses that everyone's heard before. Feign confidence, look your boss straight in the eye and opt for one of the following approaches:

BRAZEN
'Late? I've been here the whole time!'

FEY
'Outside the office I was suddenly struck by the sheer beauty of this world, and stood paralysed with rapture for 45 minutes, watching a bird try to eat a gummy bear.'

SLICK
'I'm working on New York time.'

MENACING

'I was taken in for questioning on suspicion of murder.'

BROWN-NOSING

'I was busy being headhunted by [*insert name of rival company*]. I turned them down, because I am TOO LOYAL to you, but then had to comfort them for two hours.'

UNIMPEACHABLE

'I want you to listen to me. I'm going to say this again: I did NOT have sexual relations with that woman.'

Alice from St Mary Hoo, Kent: While waiting in line for the Saw ride at Thorpe Park, the pondlife couple in front of me started full-on groping each other. You could see her hand down his trousers while she was tossing him off. . . WHY? What is it that would turn you on about being in a queue?

Like you, Alice, we don't feel stirrings in our loins as we stand in line at the post office or wait our turn at the bank. This couple, however, is made of more enterprising stuff. They're not going to resort to the typical time-whiling entertainments of shuffling, sighing, or texting, because they've gone to Thorpe Park for a day of fun, goddammit, and the fun doesn't start when they set foot on the ride: the fun starts RIGHT NOW.

They might also have been turned on by the prospect of the scary rollercoaster ahead – fear can be a powerful aphrodisiac, pumping adrenalin round the body, which is why even as they flee from near-certain horrible death, characters in films still find the time for a quickie. Alternatively, this couple might have anticipated that the gore of Saw will be a total passion-killer, so they'd better get their rocks off beforehand. There's method in their madness: that ride involves some extremely fast plunges. If she were to grasp his member at the wrong moment, she could snap it clean off.

Stephen: What is the point of a tie (i.e. a neck tie)? I admit that they make people feel and look more smart, but WHY? What is their function?

There are myriad functions of a tie, Stephen! A jokey cartoon-patterned one proves to your colleagues that you *do* have a personality after all, albeit one that could do with a lot of work. A stripy one tells everyone that you attended Eton, were a school prefect, or are a member of a gentleman's club, and as you're trumpeting that fact far more publicly than necessary, they should avoid chatting to you at a wedding reception. A pale-yellow leather tie worn with a dark shirt suggests you were in the original cast of *Neighbours*. A bow tie signals that you're a gynaecologist, magician or Pee-wee Herman.

Ties also have aesthetic purposes. A long vertical stripe of colour down one's middle can have a slimming, elongating effect upon the gent who worries he has become a little broad in the beam. For men who have to dress in suits much of the time, the tie is the one part of their respectable business ensemble with which they can have a bit of fun, and wear a colour that isn't grey, blue or black. And a tie is an inexpensive way to pep up the same old outfit – just look at Jon Snow on the nightly news over the course of a week to understand how effectively the same suit can be reinvented with a diaspora of neckwear.

It's handy to have a tie on you for emergencies, too, should you need a makeshift tourniquet or bandage following a horrible motorway pile-up, or a headband lest an impromptu game of Ninjas breaks out at the office. In fact, the tie was born as a purely practical device. Shirts used to be loose-fitting garments without buttons, so the neck was kept closed with a long strip of cloth. Men were dandier back then, never resistant to an opportunity for extra decoration, hence this cloth evolved into bows, frills, ruffs and cravats.

The arrival of the Industrial Revolution prompted the need for more functional, comfortable, less froufrou neckwear, because if you were busy all day pumping the spinning jenny or whatever, you didn't have the time to check that your ruff was still in peak condition. Thus the modern-style long thin tie was invented, and anyone who doesn't like them is therefore a neo-Luddite. We presume that was the underlying message of your question, Stephen; and no, we're not going to help you smash up any steam engines.

Polly from Brick Lane: Why do conversations about baby names always go on much longer than other boring and speculative conversations?

Babies brew for nine sodding months, so expectant parents are understandably impatient. They yearn to talk about their spawn, but are hamstrung by lack of material because they haven't even met the wee bairn yet.

Non-parental participants are just as much to blame for propagating these conversations. The name of the impending baby is a comparatively harmless avenue about which to enquire, unlikely to result in a response that is nauseatingly biological, emotionally volatile, or something tedious about local primary schools. Would you really rather have a long, boring and speculative conversation about perineal tears? The afterbirth? Piles? Thought not. Now buckle up and try to look interested.

Olly says:

In 1981, a boring and speculative conversation about baby names saved my bacon.

My dad sells vintage Bentleys for a living, and throughout my childhood 'encouraged' me, constantly and blatantly, to become excited about his profession, which tragically for him I never was. At primary school I gave a speech about vintage Bentleys, entirely ghostwritten by him. I had my own little toy Bentley that I drove around the house. I even had Bentley wallpaper.

All of this was fair game, really – most fathers attempt to influence their children's life choices, and the fact that I was always more interested in musicals than Formula One demonstrates that the brainwashing wasn't too intensive. However. I've since discovered that, had my mother not decisively nixed the scheme whilst I was still safely tucked up in her womb, *I was going to be called Bentley*.

I dread to think how that would have been abbreviated in the playground. Bendy Mann? Bent Mann? BENDER? So many options, all of them insulting. And what could this Bentley Mann possibly go on to do for a living, apart from perform gangsta rap, or manage a residential home for elderly homosexuals? He certainly wouldn't sell Bentleys, for fear of becoming a parody of himself, so the decision to name him after the marque would have been entirely counterproductive.

Thanks, Mum. I owe you one.

Miranda from Suffolk: How long is it acceptable or polite to keep birthday cards displayed after the big day?

We think two weeks is an acceptable length of time. Once the cards are collapsing under the weight of dust, it's time to retire them to your keepsake drawer.

Richard from Exeter: I've been stuck in a traffic pile-up for an hour and a half and I'm desperate for a wee. Is it acceptable to get out of the car and go at the side of the road?

It's OK, provided the spectacle of your al fresco urination does not cause another pile-up.

Claire: I have an English interview at Oxford University tomorrow, and am simultaneously excited and, quite frankly, SHITTING MYSELF. So Helen and Olly, as fully-fledged Oxford English graduates, answer me this: what sort of questions popped up at your interviews, and do you have any pearls of wisdom for all us nervous university applicants out there?

Like youth hostelling and Sir Patrick Moore, no one expected Oxford interviews to survive into the twenty-first century. The process of selection seems so secretive, so subjective, so arbitrary; a lucky dip of eccentrics standing between each straight-A student and a place at one of the world's most prestigious tourist attractions. To successfully charm these elderly oddballs, you need to be a) super-brainy, b) from an extremely rich family, or c) brimming with chutzpah. We'll let you conclude which category we were in.

We don't recall precise questions that came up in our interviews, but they were in all likelihood pretty straightforward:

'Why do you want to study here?'; 'Which authors do you like to read?'; 'What's your favourite Anglo-Saxon rhyme scheme?' and so on. What we do remember are the tutors' responses: 'How *very* pedestrian!'; 'I'd hardly call that *literature*!'; 'Are you wasting our time?'; 'Explain that again, as if to a tiny stupid child!' and so on. They seemed to be testing our ability to deflect abuse rather than answer questions, which is perhaps why Oxbridge proves such a reliable training ground for a career in politics.

Just for you, Claire, here is our potted guide to sailing through that interview process:

- If asked how you feel about having to read Old and Middle English, Literary Theory and Epic Poetry, LIE.
- Any literature written since 1965 does not exist. Women authors do not exist, not even Jane Austen or any of the Brontës. Iris Murdoch is an exception, because she was from Oxford, and didn't look too girly.
- Girls: if in a tight spot, BURST INTO TEARS. We met loads of people who got into Oxford after doing this.
- Boys: be absurdly polite. Imagine Richard Curtis invented you.
- If the tutor makes a joke, laugh.
- If the tutor makes a pass at you, don't laugh.
- Some colleges invite you to stay over the night before your interview. This provides an opportunity to spend an evening with your fellow interviewees. This is good. It also provides an opportunity to get wasted, dump a supermarket trolley in the quad and defecate on a statue of William Wordsworth. This is bad.
- Don't base your analysis of Dickens or Shakespeare on musical adaptations. You will be rumbled.

Sonny: Why do so many girls describe themselves as 'dumb blondes'? Do they feel it makes them more attractive to men? Do they not think it makes them look more like slags?

See there, Sonny, you've just done the very thing which is encouraging this behaviour in Team Blonde: associating blondeness with slagginess. These fair-headed ladies have grown used to this widely held assumption, so their self-deprecation is just a pre-emptive strike upon the stereotype they can't escape. Don't imagine they aren't being cunning, however: they're also keeping your expectations low so that when they start dissecting Heisenberg's Uncertainty Principle, your jaw will drop so far that it bashes you in the testicles on the way down.

Angela: When having afternoon tea with friends, is it appropriate to cut off the crusts of the sandwiches or (as they are friends) would it be acceptable to leave them on?

We are surely not the only people who actually prefer our sandwiches to have crusts. So, unless your friends are babies or nonagenarians, leave them on. If you really aspire for your event to emulate the experience of tea at the Ritz, ban flash photography and charge your friends a pound to use the loo.

Mik: A while ago my sperm turned bright red. A little worried, I called my doctor. She told me not to worry – it was caused by overactive sex (lucky girlfriend) and would gradually disappear. To keep a check I was told to wank into a condom every day and compare results. After about a week, and feeling pleased at my now healing sperm, we all had a good night on the town, returning to my place to carry the party on. The question is this: did I get out my condoms filled with various shades of spunk too early to show everyone? The party atmosphere seemed to lose its direction after that.

It is so hard, isn't it, to navigate one's way through modern-day social mores. Is it still frowned upon to drink cappuccino after dinner? Is it OK to serve shop-bought pre-mixed cocktails? When *is* the right time to show your friends a collection of your blood-tinged semen? Oh, how we wish we had gone to finishing school when we had the chance!

We're sure of one thing, at least: if you'd left the room telling everyone you were just going to fetch some nibbles, we can understand why the festivities took a sharp turn for the worse when you returned with your rainbow of bodily fluids.

Alex: Where is the best place to fall asleep in public? Where is the worst place to fall asleep in public?

OLLY:

Best: on a beach. But, if you have a sentimental attachment to your belongings, not a beach in Italy.

Worst: watching the opening act of any Shakespeare play which you haven't read in advance. Waking up halfway through, you have zero chance of following the plot, yet might have to endure a further two hours before you can leave.

HELEN:

Best: in one of the comfy chairs at the library. So peaceful and quiet, so warm and airless. But try not to snore.

Worst: at university, in a one-on-one tutorial with a world expert on my subject. Yes, he did notice. No, he was not forgiving.

? *Robert from Florida: When my girlfriend and I are lying together in bed, how can I pass gas without her noticing?*

Olly's favoured technique is to lie on his side, arsehole pointing away from his girlfriend. From this position he is able to casually slip his left hand down his pyjamas. By gently massaging one arse-cheek away from the other, ensuring his sphincter is tightly regulated, he has found it possible to slowly psssssst out a gaseous whisper without disturbing his other half. But if a real rumble in the jungle is brewing, he finds his best tactic is to wait until she goes to the bathroom, whereupon he can lift his legs high above his head and parp as quickly and violently as possible before she returns to slumberland.

So now you know. And now you wish you hadn't asked.

Rick from East Dulwich: I'm going on a cruise with Mum and Dad. They've briefed me that I have to get dolled up in a dinner suit. I have worn a dinner suit only four times in my life, and don't understand the etiquette and social statements you make with the choices you make. So, answer me these:

Proper bow tie or pre-tied?
Pre-tied. It's much less suave-looking, but you're a novice at the dinner suit malarkey, and bow tie-tying is for black belts only.
Patterned/spotted or plain?
Plain. Black. Anything else will mark you out as 'The wacky guy!' and nobody wants to be stuck on a boat with him.
Wing collar or flat collar?
Whichever one doesn't make you feel like you're choking.
Patent shoes or suede shoes?
Patent. If you're seasick, you'll never get the stains out of suede.
Cummerbund or waistcoat?

If you're a bit tubby at the beginning of the cruise, wear a cummerbund. After two weeks on board, eating seven meals a day because there's nothing else to do, upsize to a waistcoat. Keep a kaftan in emergency reserve.

Kimon from Corfu: Why do people who are getting married suddenly want ice-cream makers?

They don't really. Nor do they want bread-makers, USB photo-frames, a 24-place setting of silver cutlery, a soup tureen, or a teppanyaki hotplate. They just want Stuff. You see, while many freshly-betrothed couples confidently take the stance that wedding lists are grabby and wrong and they're not going to have one, most reverse their position as soon as they discover the cost per guest of the reception. If they're paying £80 for you to sit on a gold-painted chair eating under-seasoned lamb shank and sugared almonds, they're damn well going to recoup it in kind.

Quite what to ask for, however, is trickier than it used to be in the days when couples didn't live together until they were married and therefore relied upon the wedding list to accrue all the tea-towels, bathmats, toasters and fish kettles required for matrimony. Listing things one genuinely wants can seem rather too revealing – a riding crop, size 13 stilettos, a subscription to *What Caravan?* – or too utilitarian to be sufficiently festive – a year's supply of paper towels, a kilo of bicarbonate of soda, 100 pairs of Marks and Spencer underpants. Which is how you end up asking for items that are unlikely ever to make it out of the packaging, let alone into service.

To be fair, many couples do feel awkward about asking, just as guests feel resentful to be asked. Perhaps, Kimon, the wider world should institute a custom from your native Greece, where instead of buying boring things off a list lodged at John Lewis, guests pin cash onto the bride and groom. Everybody would benefit: hard currency would be considerably more useful to the couple than luxury kitchen equipment, while the guests would find their obligation to shell out far more palatable in the guise of a fairground-style game with the potential for minor blood spillage.

Tibi from London: I do CCF at school and we had to shine our army boots for Remembrance Sunday. Why do they get us to do that? I think it looks stupid.

Cuff that insolent boy around the lughole! The shinification of an army boot has implications on many levels, primarily because paying your respects to late soldiers seems much less respectful if you turn up looking like a big scruffbag.

Everyone's seen enough bossy sergeants in war films to know that in the army, details count. They're trying to unify a raggle-taggle bunch of young bucks, and they need to instil discipline – if they start the soldiers off with small things, for instance by regulating the tucking of bedsheets, then later they'll be far less likely to forget their ammo or face the wrong direction when they reach the Front. Also, if you can't even maintain the toes of your boots to a decent standard, it doesn't say much for your maintenance of more important things like your tanks and armoured helicopters. The enemy will look down at your footwear – especially if they're Italian – and titter in your face, before lobbing a hand grenade down your trousers.

There's another reason that you had to do this, Tibi. School have got to keep you busy for a whole afternoon in CCF, and there's only so much time you can fill with marching, saluting, cleaning mess-tins and smearing your face in camouflage paint. It's better that they make you shine your boots than send you off for a tour of Afghanistan.

It all depends upon what job you're applying for. The selection procedures for hedge funding and hedge trimming differ wildly. It also depends upon what sort of interviewee you are, Nathan from Battersea, so take our quiz to ascertain this and then we can tailor our advice for impressiveness to your especial characteristics. GO:

HELEN AND OLLY'S MULTIPLE CHOICE INTERVIEW QUIZ

Why do you want to work for our organisation?
a) I see your company as the best in your field.
b) My girlfriend says she'll leave me if I don't get a job.
c) If you don't give me the job, you'd better sleep with one eye open. That's all I'm saying.

What's your biggest fault?
a) Perfectionism.
b) I snore when I've smoked too much weed.
c) Killing.

Do you work well in a team?
a) Yes! I was vice-captain of the school netball squad.
b) Well, a lot of the stuff I watch online involves groups.
c) I tend to work best alone, or perhaps with one accomplice.

Why did you leave your last job?
a) I felt it was time for a new challenge.
b) We disagreed on whether Tuesday still counted as the weekend.
c) I am prohibited from being within one hundred yards of the building.

Answer Me This!

159

Where do you see yourself in five years' time?

a) Working hard, playing hard, and hopefully doing my best for this company.

b) In Goa, working on my music.

c) Hiding in your wardrobe, waiting for you to come home.

I see there's a gap in your CV. What were you doing in those two years after university?

a) Voluntary work in Africa, building a cottage hospital and picking up valuable life skills.

b) Shit, that was TWO YEARS? I thought I only lost a week!

c) Allow me to refer you to the true-crime movie *Another Girl Gone.*

What are your training and development needs?

a) I'm a bit rusty with Excel, but I'm a quick learner, and love to pick up new skills.

b) I have to retake my driving test once my three-year ban's over.

c) Gaffer tape and a hammer.

RESULTS

Nathan, if you scored mostly As: you are a very solid candidate, but a bit of a snore. You need to find a way to stand out from the other 30 interviewees giving the same answers as you, but we fear you may lack the personality to do it. You'd better wear your most humorous socks, and flash a bit of ankle.

If you scored mostly Bs: you display a very relaxed attitude to corporate life, and a lot of stressed executives could learn from you. Suggest to the interviewer that you carve yourself a niche in the company as the workplace wellbeing manager. Drop a small amount of your 'party supplies' into the coffee machine and that's your job done.

If you scored mostly Cs: you don't need our help. You need a top-notch legal team, a knife sharpener, and a very discreet and hardworking cleaner.

Mark from Brighton: When sitting in a café in India, I was surprised to hear people openly discussing their bowel movements in indescribably frank detail. When does it become acceptable to discuss the otherwise unacceptable like it's the weather?

Most likely the chaps Mark overheard were teenagers on gap years. Teens tend to be incredibly introspective, which is why all the language used to advertise these expeditions – 'find yourself', 'broaden your horizons', 'have an experience' – focus on *them*, and have sod all to do with the beleaguered backwater they've chosen as their destination. It shouldn't come as a surprise, therefore, that when they land overseas their observations continue to be all about themselves and their bodies, and seldom about the undernourished unfortunates who actually live there.

Olly was guilty of this himself, aged 18 and on a trip in troubled Zimbabwe, where he spent more time chatting to his travel companions about the state of his guts than Mugabe's murderous mismanagement of the country. This created a state of heightened familiarity with his fellow explorers which eventually evolved into the utter abandonment of all conventional etiquette. At one point, he even failed to recognise that the locals might consider it objectionable if he briefly decamped from a tour bus to take a dump in someone's front garden. On another occasion, he suffered such shooting, spouting diarrhoea that it splattered his socks with luminescent yellow stains. Such was his physical, mental and social decrepitude that he didn't even bother cleaning off the evidence, and walked around town with vibrant seepage on his legs, so intimate were his companions with the ever-changing status of each other's anal spewage. So Mark, consider yourself lucky to have got off so lightly with just an earful.

? *Tom: I recently had an important meeting with a Distinguished Gentleman in a café, and I noticed he had spilt cappuccino down his jumper. Should I have told him before he went to his next meeting?*

A tricky one, this. Had he left his flies open, you would definitely be best to remain silent, lest he conclude you had been gazing at his groin. Had a crumb of croissant clung to his moustache, you should notify him, because he'd be grateful to know he'd been walking about with pastry on his face. But a stained jumper presents a dilemma. Tell him, and you could come across as observant and compassionate – two useful qualities to demonstrate in an important meeting. On the other hand, the outcome could be undesirable, because the balance of power in the meeting would be disrupted, and he would subconsciously hold you responsible for the whole debacle. There's not much he can do to repair the damage except attempt to dab the coffee off with a damp napkin, which would embarrass him and further expand the wet patch.

Your best option would be to deliberately sabotage your own jumper with cappuccino. When you look down and exclaim, 'Damn, I ALWAYS do that!', the distinguished gentleman will mirror your actions, glance down his own front and spot his own spillage, yet feel unabashed to have echoed your error. Then, as he left the café for his next meeting he'd be thinking, 'That young Tom, he's like a less distinguished version of me! What a guy.'

Dave from Coventry: Why do some people (mainly middle-aged men) feel the need to wear their Bluetooth earpiece ALL the time, for example in a supermarket or whilst having a meal out with their family? I think it's because they're either very rude or are pretending that they actually know other people.

Frankly, at their age, they don't care what you think. Assuming they didn't simply forget they were still wearing it – which is the most probable reason – they sport it to express that despite their age they are hip, contemporary and still fully capable of kicking it with the funky bunch. Remember, this telecommunications revolution entered their world at precisely the same moment they began to buy their trainers from Marks and Spencer and stopped drinking coffee because they don't know the difference between a Frappuccino and a Filipino.

Our favourite proponent of the visible earpiece trend phenomenon is our friend Sam's father, who wears exclusively beige, presumably because it doesn't show up dandruff. So devoted to this colour scheme is he that he actually *painted his Bluetooth headset beige* to match the rest of his outfits. Middle-aged men 1, fashion police 0.

David in Maldon: How come my 13-year-old daughter can spend hours getting her hair and makeup just perfect, but her room always looks like an explosion that blew up a branch of Claire's Accessories inside a New Look store? How can I make her keep her room tidy?

Ah, David, have you forgotten what it is to be young? It might look like a mess to you, but no doubt your daughter knows *exactly* where everything in her room is, and to tidy up would only be, in her eyes, to secrete all the stuff she actually needs under a big pile of crap that she doesn't. This is why *Mary Poppins* resonates with generations of children. Your daughter dreams of the day her room would clean itself with a simple click of her fingers, leaving her free to go to the bank, fly a kite and let a mucky cockney take her up the chimney.

The notion that you can 'make her' keep her room tidy is as flawed as preventing a dog from fouling the pavement by wedging a cork up its arse: the harder you block the flow, the fiercer the explosion will be. Teenagers are natural rebels, programmed to resist their parents' every command, and even if you did succeed in bribing her into action, she would only ram everything into a cupboard or under the bed anyway.

Just sit tight, and don't lose hope. Eventually – admittedly not for another five years or so – she will realise for herself that the bin is a better place for a rotting packed lunch than her bedside table. She might even go super-tidy: for reasons scientists have yet to explain, by her early thirties she may develop the Soft Furnishings gene, after which she will not consider a room to be visitor-ready unless it contains a perfectly aligned row of neutral cushions, a poster of 'Le Chat Noir' and a vase full of pine cones.

***Eliot and Lexie from Chesham**: Why mustn't you wake sleepwalkers when they're sleepwalking?*

If you find your boyfriend roaming the kitchen at 3 a.m. with a glassy expression on his face, talking in nonsensical mumbles, you've either got a sleepwalker on your hands, or you live with George Michael. In each case, it can be pretty scary, so it should come as no surprise that the guidelines for partners of sleepwalkers sound like they're lifted from *Dawn of the Dead*: install a gate at the top of stairs so they can't fall down; lock your doors and windows so they can't jump out; shoot them straight in the face to prevent them feasting on human flesh.

When it comes to waking them up, popular opinion is divided, but there is scientific consensus that the dangers are overstated. Sleepwalkers become confused if woken, and might briefly suffer a small spasm of shock, so it's best to lead them gently back to bed by the elbow. But if you wake them up with a Party Popper or a bucket of cold water, they'll probably survive, and the world will thank you for some jolly YouTube fodder. Besides, if you've prevented them from jumping out of a third-storey window, or taking a shit in the wardrobe, they should be very grateful.

Hamish from Edinburgh: What are your favourite euphemisms?

PHRASE	MEANING
It's not you, it's me . . .	It's you.
Love the show!	Please read out my letter on the radio
I adored this project from the moment I read the script.	My third wife really cleaned me out.
I have a few issues with emotion.	I am damaged goods. Run!
Have you had an injury in the workplace that wasn't your fault?	Are you gullible?
Go fuck yourself, fag!	I prefer other videos on YouTube to this one.

Rob from Bedford: I am getting married later this year. I fear that the emotion of the day may get to me and I might start to well up as my fiancée walks down the aisle towards me. (These will be tears of joy, not fear (probably).) How can I avoid breaking down and looking like an idiot?

No one will think you're an idiot if you cry. We think it's marvellous to see a man in touch with his emotions, especially on such an important day, and it would be a shame if he felt he had to suppress them. Helen's brother blubbed helplessly throughout his own wedding speech, despite being utterly composed and in full control of his faculties at all other times; and accordingly, in a crowd full of professional cynics, there was not a dry eye in the house.

But, if you're absolutely set on emotional stonewalling, you'll have to distract yourself, in much the same manner as when you prevent yourself from reaching sexual climax by thinking about genocide, or Ann Widdecombe, or Ann Widdecombe committing genocide. Summon up an image that makes you angry: one can't easily weep with joy during an internal rant about speed cameras, the cost of having your boiler serviced, or the existence of all eight series of *Two Pints of Lager and a Packet of Crisps*.

If such mental gymnastics fail to stem the flow of tears, ensure nobody attributes them to sentiment by creating a smokescreen. Produce a raw onion from your jacket pocket and bite into it. Or attack the congregation with pepper spray so that everyone else is crying too. Your special day will be truly unforgettable.

Callum: Did you have any ridiculous rules at school? We aren't allowed to drink water from anything but a clear plastic bottle!

HELEN: My secondary school had an 80-page rule book. It had only recently started admitting girls, so I'm guessing some of the weirder clauses were designed as much to keep the veteran teachers from bubbling over after a lifetime in the company of men as they were to keep our adolescent hormones suppressed.

A straitlaced maths teacher called Mrs Johnson elected herself the chief warden of our feminine wiles. Our uniform was a baggy kilt in Black Watch tartan, until we entered the sixth form, whereupon we had to wear tight grey pencil skirts instead. Mrs Johnson carried a tape measure with which she performed spot checks to ensure that the skirts' hemlines were no more than two inches above the knee. Her precautions were wasted, as the aforementioned tightness meant that if you bounded up a flight of stairs, the skirts would split along the back seam right up to the gusset.

Mrs Johnson's best rule didn't last long in the statute books, but by Jove, it was a corker: girls were not allowed to eat bananas unless they were sliced up first. Judging by the perennially furious red face of Mr Johnson, the school librarian, he may have suffered the same fate at home.

OLLY: At my primary school, you weren't allowed to wear trousers unless you were taller than 4 foot 11; shorties were stuck wearing shorts. This bizarre rule resulted in a trouser-based hierarchy, as gargantuan eight-year-olds bullied anyone who was older but shorter. Yet the headmaster wore a full-length suit, even though he can't have been taller than 4 foot 8. Hypocrite!

Leroy from Scotland: I Have A Stalker. And . . . I Really Mean A Stalker. This Guy TOLD Me He Was Obsessed With Me And Got So Attached That I Ended Up Having To Run Away From Him And Avoid Him. Every Time I Turn Around, He Is There . . . Watching Me. I Offered To Do Up His Bebo For Him Because His Was Rubbish . . . And His Password Was My Name!! He Even Went To The Extent Of Writing His Phone Number On A Pizza Box For Me (He Works In Dominoes). And Get This . . . When I Ordered A Chinese Take-Out The Other Night He Text Me Saying 'Enjoying Your Chinese?' So Answer Me This – HOW THE HELL DO I GET HIM TO STOP?!?!

To be honest, Leroy, your overuse of capital letters makes *you* look a bit psycho. Did you cut words out of newspaper headlines and paste them into your question?

Furthermore, we cannot fathom what you were thinking when you helped him with his Bebo. Your fear of this chap must be outweighed by your aversion to an inadequate Bebo page; because if *we* were being targeted by an ardent stalker (and chance would be a fine thing), we would not be fanning the flames of his/her misplaced devotion by helpfully assisting him/her with an entirely non-essential task.

Instead, we would first try having a little word with our stalker, something along the lines of, 'Now look here, old bean, this won't do, what what?' Then we would back up our words with action, by doing our level best to avoid all contact with them. You must avert your eyes from his gaze. Do not smile in his presence, or do anything which he could possibly manage to interpret as encouragement. Do NOT offer to help him scrub his back. And, much as this may hurt, find yourself an alternative pizza supplier.

If necessary, make yourself scarce for a while. Scotland has many excellent hiding-places, just ask an English monarch from the Middle Ages.

Tim: What's the optimal length for a handshake?

Enough time to clasp hands, shake thrice and release. Any less makes the other person believe you find their paw too repulsive to touch for a nanosecond longer; any more and it might develop into a full-on recreation of the wrestling scene from *Women in Love*.

Amy from Maidenhead: At what age does it become inappropriate to need to sleep with a soft toy? Aged almost 18, I can't help thinking that I should have probably grown out of this ten years ago. It has got to the stage where I must take Pandie, my one-armed panda, to my boyfriend's house when I stay over. Naturally, he does seem to get in the way as I have to keep him in bed (Pandie that is, not my boyfriend), but if I put him by the side of the bed I feel as though he's perving on me.

At almost 18, you are teetering on the fulcrum of age-appropriateness. So long as you refrain from other pseudo-childish tendencies, such as sucking your thumb or speaking in a baby voice, your continued attachment to Pandie could still count as quite cute. But in the coming years, you must start weaning yourself off. You might be able to get away with it at university, claiming the allegiance is a twenty-first-century tribute to Sebastian Flyte; but by the time you hit your thirties, being constantly accompanied by Pandie will not only mark you out as a madwoman, but also seriously impede your romantic and sexual relationships.

From your question, it appears that is already happening. If even you are finding randy Pandie offputting during moments of passion, imagine what it's doing to your boyfriend! Granted, most men mid-performance won't even be distracted by the eruption of Mount Etna next door; but if we were your boyfriend, we would find Pandie to be a kapok-stuffed cockblocker.

Therefore, we prescribe a gradual programme of dePandification. Start by turning Pandie to face the wall, so that your romps are no longer haunted by his unblinking plastic stare. The next stage is propping him just outside the bedroom door; or, to keep him entertained, pop him in front of the telly in the living room. You'll soon be ready to graduate to leaving him at home; although to ease the pain of this adjustment, you could carry a small memento of him with you – maybe a photo, or better yet, keep his detached arm in your handbag for whenever you need a Pandie fix.

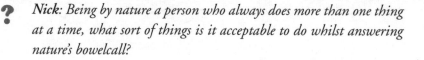

Nick: Being by nature a person who always does more than one thing at a time, what sort of things is it acceptable to do whilst answering nature's bowelcall?

1. Read a six-month-old copy of a magazine that you don't like enough to read at any other time;
2. Draw smiley faces on your knees with a biro.
   THAT IS ALL.

The Odditorium

Oozing out of the dank dungeon beneath the *Answer Me This!* question library, here are the questions to which you never knew you wanted the answers.

George: How many people must one kill before it is classed as a spree?

According to the US Bureau of Justice Statistics, who make it their business to know such things, you would need to kill a minimum of two people, in more than one location, but in a short period of time. Even if you spread your kills over a couple of days, you must perform them during one single burst of psychotic rage, because proper spree killers do NOT allow themselves down-time until their work is done. So no stopping to chill out, George, unless you want to be classified as a common-or-garden serial killer.

Damian from South Wales: Could you make black pudding out of menstrual blood?

You could. But that doesn't mean you should.

Pappy: What does a unicorn's dick feel like?

It very much depends what position you're in.

Chris: *How the fuck do you get out of the Crystal Palace Maze?*

Oh come *on*, Chris. Despite being the biggest maze in London, Crystal Palace Maze is also the easiest. And it has an escape path straight to the exit. If you're too useless to find that, then man up and gnaw your way out.

Eleanor, Frankie and Rachel from St Albans: *Why does the Falklands flag have a sheep on top of a ship on it?*

The ship represents the good ship *Desire*, in which top Elizabethan explorer John Davis accidentally discovered the Falklands in 1592, on a disastrous voyage during which most of his crew died from eating rotten penguins, and not of the McVitie's variety. The sheep teetering incongruously above the ship symbolises the Falklands' favourite pastime: sheep-farming. As for why the sheep is absolutely gigantic compared to the ship, that's easily explained: it's drawn from the perspective of someone looking out to sea by peering through the legs of a sheep, which is the prerogative of a flag artist.

OUR 10 FAVOURITE WORLD FLAGS, INTERPRETED

1. Qatar
Keep your ticket stub to gain re-entry.

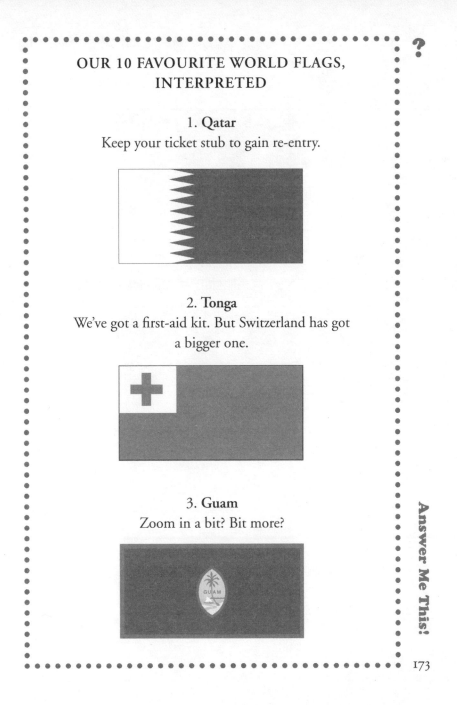

2. Tonga
We've got a first-aid kit. But Switzerland has got a bigger one.

3. Guam
Zoom in a bit? Bit more?

4. Malawi
Peekaboo!

5. Norfolk Island
Come to Norfolk Island! It's Christmas every day.

6. Gibraltar
We Heart ClipArt.

7. Uganda

We're going to take you down, Nando's . . .

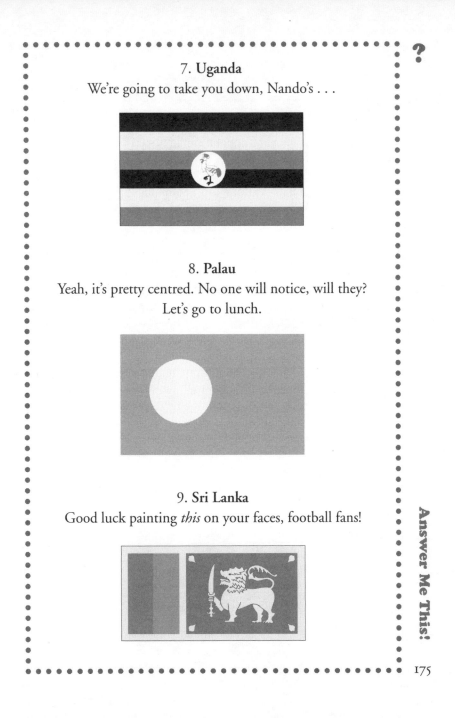

8. Palau

Yeah, it's pretty centred. No one will notice, will they?
Let's go to lunch.

9. Sri Lanka

Good luck painting *this* on your faces, football fans!

10. Libya

Seriously now, this was the best you could come up with?

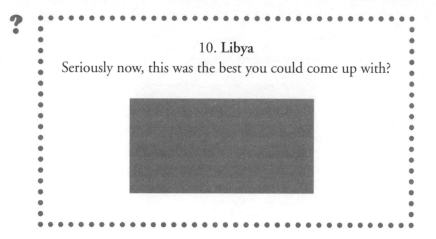

Calvin: With so many French people arriving in the UK, and with the UK having such crap weather, why don't we do country swapsies?

They tried that before in 1066, but it proved unpopular.

Holly from Guildford: Does the phrase 'He who smelt it dealt it' stand up in a court of law?

No, but the phrase 'The one who said the rhyme did the crime' does. Which is why Her Majesty's Prisons are overcrowded with performance poets.

Elliot from Buckinghamshire: Who first coined the phrase 'get in', and what does it mean?

1. A prick. 2. 'I'm a prick!'

Neale from Leeds: Do snakes have arseholes, and if so, where? Because I don't think I've ever seen one with an arse.

First of all, Neale, you should really stop ogling snakes. It's rude.

Anyway, snakes do have anuses, just like other beasts; they just don't feel the need to flash them about as cats do. They keep them tucked away on their undersides, a few inches from their pointy end; and given how they don't tend to spend a load of time lolling about on their backs, the only way you're likely to catch sight of one is by covering a glass coffee table with snakes, then lying underneath it with a magnifying glass waiting for the money shot.

Josh from London: Do you happen to know what that little pocket inside the larger pocket on jeans is for? It's pointless. A friend of mine suggested it could be for change, but I can't get change out after I've put it in.

We refer you to Michel Gondry's award-winning Levi's advert. In this monochrome mini-movie, set in Depression-era America, a chiselled young chap wearing a pair of 501s visits his local pharmacy for a packet of rubber johnnies. This shocks his fellow customers, but not the cheeky pharmacist, who nods in tacit advocacy. Mr 501 stuffs his prophylactics into the tiniest pocket of his jeans and drives off to pick up his date. But, her father opens the door and . . . why, he is none other than the cheeky pharmacist! That sure wipes the smile off his face, because now he realises his precious daughter is about to get fucked. Ha ha ha. Finally, the slogan: 'Watch pocket created in 1873. Abused ever since.'

So there you have it. The trouser feature originally designed as a watch pocket by Levi Strauss is not for your small change, but for FUN.

Emma from Ireland: What are bulletproof vests made of and how do they work?

Like the vests our grannies used to knit for us, they are made from tight layers of strong ballistic fibres which deform speeding bullets and absorb their force, thus preventing them from penetrating your flesh and generally ruining your afternoon. The military use more sophisticated vests, augmented with metal – but there's no point getting cold nipples unless you know you're going to get showered with some serious shrapnel.

But there's no guarantee a bulletproof vest will be fully bulletproof. Borrowing terminology from 'water-resistant' raincoats that are as resistant to a light spring drizzle as Jennifer Aniston is to accepting parts in indistinguishable romantic comedies, the vests are often sold as 'bullet-resistant'. Though when one fails, the victim isn't in much of a state to take it back to the shop for a refund.

Dan: Why is the hard shoulder of a motorway called 'the hard shoulder'?

Because if it were called 'the paved appendage' it would make all news reports about car crashes sound unintentionally effete.

Kathryn from Denver: Why do they give out bouquets to medal winners during the Olympics?

'Congratulations, great athlete! Finally, it has arrived, the moment you have dreamt of all your life, the incentive for all those 4a.m. training sessions jogging up a rain-lashed hill with a tractor tyre tied to your waist, the mental picture that stopped you from throwing up your daily elevenses of raw egg-whites: I'm putting a medal round your neck! A shiny, heavy, real metal medal. Every last one of your countrymen is teary with love for you, and you're now a role model for all children. History will

The Odditorium

remember you forever, standing proud on this rostrum, medal glinting against your tracksuit top, perspiration drying on your face into a triumphant glow.

'But hang on, your hands are looking awfully empty. Better do something about that, quick. Um, how about I present you with this oversized teddy bear? No, no, too silly for such an important victory . . . Perhaps a big box of chocolates? Whoops, of course not, not for you health-conscious sportsperson, you! Forgive me. Would a mug look sufficiently celebratory? Muscle-soothing bubble bath? A book token? Of course you don't care for reading. Dearie me, it's always hard buying gifts for people you don't know very well, isn't it?

'In that case, you must accept this three-foot-long bunch of flowers. Why, I insist! Look, I'm sure they'll let you take them home in your hand luggage. Just ask nicely, OK? Shut up and take them, right, because they'll look good in the photos, and frankly, their scent is currently the only thing stopping everyone from keeling over from the sweaty pong of your prize-winning exertions. Take them. TAKE THEM! Plant them in the long jump afterwards, I don't even frigging care any more. If you don't shut your mouth, hold up the flowers and shed a patriotic tear, I'm going to make damn sure your piss tests positive for steroids. Just you try me.'

Mark from Essex: Why doesn't superglue stick to the inside of the tube?

It only hardens when it comes into contact with air. Those clever glue-scientists think of everything! Or at least they thought of the one thing that meant their product wasn't doomed straight out of the gate.

Because nothing says 'Welcome to my world, won't you come on in' like a wee ceramic Frank Dobson. And, most importantly, they *assist you with your gardening at night*. Well, so believed the nineteenth-century residents of the German town of Gräfenroda. It was here that local terracotta magnate Phillip Griebel first heard folktales about a race of green-fingered, pointy-hatted humanoids, and set about manufacturing merchandise to cash in on the stories, as if these mythical garden dwarves were a wee bearded boyband.

Soon, every home wanted one of these shit-hot figurines, and it wasn't long before English aristocrats – always to be counted upon to champion the kitsch and unappealing – shipped them over to their estates back home. Skip to the 1930s, and the little clay cretins were being mass-produced in the UK; gardens felt naked without one.

Even garden ornaments were not immune to the politics of the era, though, and it was decided not to sell them under their German name 'Gartenzwerg'. But what to call them instead? The consultation process ran and ran, like when the Post Office spent all that money rebranding themselves 'Consignia' then swiftly pretended they hadn't. Eventually the Department of Useless Objects decided that 'gnome' would be a suitable moniker, as the populace was already familiar with the word from fairytales.*

You may be blind to it, Amelia, but garden gnomes actually serve a valuable purpose, beyond keeping the rockery company. To travelling salespeople they indicate the sanity of a home-

---

* The British perception of gnomes was not as the happy horticulturists of German mythology, but ugly, bad-mannered, cave-dwelling weirdos. This explains the malicious aura exuded by the gnomes we see about the country. Or maybe they're just angry at being forced to live in caravan parks.

owner, using the same maths as when calculating the optimal number of pet cats: one or two, acceptable; three, a bit iffy; four or more: *run*!

Matthew from Colchester: Why don't badgers come out in the day?

You'd be cautious about showing your stripy face in daylight hours, Matthew from Colchester, if every time you popped out for something, a farmer tried to cull you lest you spread bovine tuberculosis to his livestock. Moreover, most badgerly foodstuffs are only available at night – they enjoy scoffing earthworms, grubs and slugs, which are at their most outgoing in the dampness of the night. Similarly, humans who only eat food from nocturnal food outlets, i.e. kebab vans, also tend to sleep all day.

Tom from Southport: Does Cat Woman eat cat food?

Nah, she's too busy clawing the sofa and licking her arsehole.

Hugo from Hereford: What is the difference between Blu-tack and White Tack?

Allow us to illustrate the differences in this table:

	Blu-Tack	White Tack
COLOUR	blue	white

Sha from Cornwell: How do Lego people have sex?

The same way we humans do: first they get legless, then they get mounted.

Clare from Archway: What is the worst thing that a stranger could find in your bin?

The first draft of our answer to this question. Sometimes we shock even ourselves.

Freyja: Is Richard Dawkins a bigot?

No, he just hates most people in the world because of what they think. He and the God of the Old Testament have a surprising amount in common.

Beth: Why do all grandmothers seem to adopt the same taste for interior design? Every grandmother's house I've ever been to harbours the same decrepit love for doilies and bland floral patterns.

Not every grandmother can be Zandra Rhodes, Beth. But even Helen's grandmother, in all other respects an absolutely classic granny, eschewed crocheted placemats in favour of bright Indian print bedspreads and cork sculptures of exotic animals. And Olly's grandma is a contemporary, minimalist Grandma 2.0 who wouldn't even deign to use a floral doily to wipe spilt Red Bull off her iPad.

Nevertheless we recognise the phenomenon you have observed, which we believe to be the decorative equivalent of Joan Collins. She's been rocking the same big-haired, padded-shouldered, brightly coloured, heavily made-up look for more than 30 years – essentially, she found her style in her heyday, and then stuck to it for ever. She wasn't going to roll with the times: really, can you imagine Joan Collins at age 60 experimenting with grunge? It's actually impossible. And she was hardly going to swallow the Nineties revival of the Seventies when she saw all that the first time around.

Similarly, grandmothers of a certain generation hit what they believed to be the pinnacle of home style in an era when chintz and fiddly bits were in, and have lived it ever since. Plus, if you're in the autumn of your life, you don't want to waste any of your valuable remaining moments in IKEA.

Silvertop: Why do birds suddenly appear every time you are near?

Because our hair looks and smells like worms.

Jason: What is the largest animal you think you could kill with your bare hands?

Hmm, let's see . . . A flea: no problem. A fish: relatively straight-forward, so long as we could put the radio on to help us pretend its last gasps were a singalong in the style of Big Mouth Billy Bass. A chicken: if we could grab hold of one, we could *just* about be convinced to break its neck, although we'd have to motivate ourselves by listening to some Eminem. A puppy? Only if we took some sedatives and cloaked its face, like a Victorian execution. And had some therapy afterwards. And that is about as far as we can imagine going: a zebra is definitely out of our league, an orca even more so. So congratulations, Jason. You've made us admit we could, probably, kill a little puppy with our bare hands. Sleep well.

Polly from Trowbridge: What are the Top Ten things to which you are indifferent?

HELEN:
1 booze
2 mayonnaise

3 Barbra Streisand

4 war movies

5 biscuits that don't have chocolate in

6 comedy panel shows

7 cats

8 Christmas cards

9 denim

10 soup

OLLY:

1 *Emmerdale*

2 tea

3 ornamental ponds

4 CNN

5 *Grease*

6 tofu

7 freckles

8 Debenhams

9 Vimto

10 cricket

Bas from East London: *If I were to piss in a Brita water filter, would it be drinkable?*

It would be no less drinkable than your unfiltered piss, but would be less likely to cause limescale build-up in your kettle should you choose to boil the piss afterwards.

Polly from Bristol: *Would the guards outside Buckingham Palace be more efficient if they looked in different directions?*

Of course they would. Indeed, if efficiency is what you're after, their whole setup needs some serious updating. It must be bloody hard to guard Her Maj to optimal standards when you're not even allowed to turn your head or swivel your eyeballs, let alone in summer when you have to do it wearing a high-necked woollen coat and a massive bearskin hat. They only stand in those narrow wooden sentry-boxes so that when they faint from heatstroke, they still remain propped upright.

It's ticklish to think that these guards – in fact some of our nation's toppest-notch soldiers – are mainstays of the English tourism industry. It pays to keep them inefficiently immobile: that way there's no danger of a blurry picture in the Facebook holiday snaps, and, as the global proliferation of human statues demonstrates, people love to look at other people not moving.

Rupert from Greenwich: If I had a standard DIY stepladder, could I fingerbang a giraffe? Or would I need a larger ladder?

A giraffe's sexy parts are only about six feet off the ground, so as long as you stretch up, you could probably complete the task without extra equipment. But if you're hoping the giraffe will give you a blowie afterwards, you'd better ask your window-cleaner for a loan of his ladder.

Charlie: What are those things called that you use to separate your shopping from someone else's on the supermarket checkout conveyor?

Charlie, Charlie, Charlie . . . We could try to find that out for you, but death from boredom is simply not how we want to go.

?

Conclusions

So, what have we learnt from all this question-answering?

- That 14-year-olds have far more complicated and demanding love lives than we ever did.
- That from birth to death, people are always fascinated by what enters and exits their stomachs.
- That there are some really stupid idioms in the English language.
- That it is remarkable most *Answer Me This!* questioneers manage to hang on to their jobs.

Although questions are potentially as endlessly varied as the humans who ask them, from our perches we observe patterns forming; having reached the end of this book, we can now offer a highly accurate analysis of the brain. Viz:

Breakdown of questioneers' preoccupations

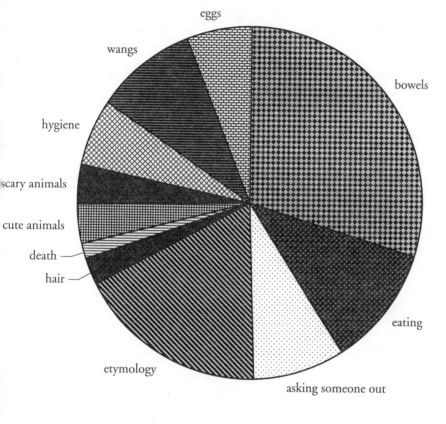

Acknowledgements

We owe boundless thanks to:

Our parents, families and friends, for their unflinching support of our silly podcasting hobby, even when it meant we missed their birthday parties because we were recording. Particular thanks are due to those friends whose most embarrassing moments we have exploited to give the world cheap laughs.

Martin Austwick, a.k.a. Martin the Sound Man, whose technical know-how and collection of microphones made *Answer Me This!* possible, and who is the orchestra-leader for our outstanding jingles (which sadly didn't translate to book form).

Jenny Robertshaw, for top-notch graphic design, and for putting up with Olly. She is made of strong stuff.

James Boggs at iTunes, saviour of podcasts.

Jonathan Conway, the greatest literary agent on this earth.

The magnificent team at Faber. We couldn't believe they took a punt on this book; and even now it's right here, a real, proper book, we still can't. Seriously, Faber, what the hell were you thinking?

Index

?

Answer Me This!

197

Answer Me This!

Index

These are the blank pages we were talking about on pages 28–9.

We still can't understand why they ruffle Alex's feathers so much.

In fact, we find them kind of soothing. A cooldown for the brain after 212 pages of intellectual aerobics.

If John Cage wrote a book, it would probably look like this.

Oh. We just checked on Amazon, and apparently John Cage *has* written a book. That's our holiday reading sorted.